EXILE IS MY TRADE

A Habib Tengour Reader

Edited & translated, with an introduction
by Pierre Joris

Black Widow Press
Boston, MA

EXILE IS MY TRADE

A Habib Tengour Reader

Black Widow Press is an imprint of Commonwealth Books, Inc., Boston, MA. Distributed to the trade by NBN (National Book Network) throughout North America, Canada, and the U.K. All Black Widow Press books are printed on acid-free paper, and glued into bindings. Black Widow Press and its logo are registered trademarks of Commonwealth Books, Inc.

Joseph S. Phillips and Susan J. Wood, Ph.D, Publishers
www.blackwidowpress.com

Cover Design: Kerrie Kemperman
Typesetting: Kerrie Kemperman
Cover art: Yves Piergeovanni, *Passe oiseau passe et apprends moi à passer* ou *le chariot de Thespis*. Pencil and gouache on kraft paper. 2001.

ISBN-13: 978-0-9842640-5-6

Printed in the United States

10 9 8 7 6 5 4 3 2 1

CONTENTS

PROSE

ESSAYS

INTRODUCTION

Born in 1947 in Mostaganem, Eastern Algeria, raised on the Arab and Berber voices of marketplace storytellers — see the two stories from his book *People of Mosta* included in this volume as an homage to his birthplace — taken to France by his parents as a pre-adolescent, Habib Tengour has lived and worked between Algeria and Paris ever since, both incarnating and, in his writing, speaking to the nomadic and (post-) colonial condition of his countrymen and -women. Trained as an anthropologist and sociologist, Tengour has taught at universities in both countries, while emerging over the years as one of the Maghrib's most forceful and visionary francophone poetic voices of the post-colonial era. Or as Jacqueline Arnaud, the great critic and holder of the first chair in Maghribian studies at the University of Paris, called him: "the major author of the second generation of Algerian immigrants." The work has the desire and intelligence to be epic, or at least to invent narrative possibilities beyond the strictures of the Western/French lyric tradition, in which his colonial childhood had schooled him.

Core to it is thus the ongoing invention of a Maghribian space for and of writing, the ongoing quest for the identification of such a space and self. For, as another Maghribian, Jacques Derrida, put it: "Autobiographical anamnesis presupposes identification. And precisely not identity. No, an identity is never given, received or attained; only the interminable and indefinitely phantasmatic process of identification endures." Or, Tengour in a kind of manifesto piece, "Maghribian Surrealism," that situates the tradition of French Surrealism as a late local variation of a much older and wider practice:

> Who is this Maghribian? How to define him?
>
> *"The woods are white or black"* despite the gone-to-earth nuances. Today definition impassions because of its implications. A domain for going astray. Political jealousy far away from the exploded sense of the true.
>
> Indeed there does exist a divided space called the Maghrib but the Maghribian is always elsewhere. And that is where he fulfills himself.
>
> Jugurtha lacked money to buy Rome.
>
> Tariq gave his name to a Spanish mountain.
>
> Ibn Khaldun found himself obliged to hand over his steed to Tamerlane.
>
> Abd el Krim corresponded with the Third International.

So let's take a closer look at this word: Maghrib. Usually given as the Arabic equivalent designating North Africa, i.e. the space today divided into four countries — Libya, Tunisia, Algeria and Morocco (though Mauritania should by rights be included too) — it also plays in Arabic as the opposite and compliment of Mashriq, the area we call the Middle East. In this sense "Maghrib" translates as the West, the place or time of sunset — mirroring the mashriq, the place where the sun rises, the East. The triconsonantal root of the word "Maghrib" is *gh-r-b*, /garaba/. From Hans Wehr's *Dictionary of Modern Written Arabic* we can gather the following cluster of meanings as offshoots of this root: "to go away, depart, absent oneself; to withdraw from, leave; to set." Now, if you do that, or if you are there, the meaning begins to list, like one of those ships Ulysses tries to get home on: "to be a stranger; to be strange, odd, queer, obscure, abstruse, difficult to comprehend." Which of course has consequences for further extensions of the word's meaning — and Wehr's entry goes on: "to depart; to leave, to go westward; to expel from the homeland, banish, exile, expatriate." This logically leads to "go to a foreign country, emigrate, to be far away from the homeland," and, obviously the farther west you go, or the more deeply you travel through it, the greater the risk to "become an occidental, become Westernized, Europeanized." All of which in due course means to "get around in the world, to see the world…" and then to "say or do a strange or amazing thing," which of course grammarians, pedants or critics may claim leads "to exceed the proper bounds, to overdo, to exaggerate," and that in turn could lead one "to laugh noisily or heartily, to guffaw." This means that exile is synonymous with West, and that to be in the West means at the same time to be in exile — wherever that West may be, in the Northern Occident or in the North African "Maghrib". So that even when you are born and live in the West = Maghrib, you are always already in the maghrib = exile.

Is it any surprise, then, that when I consulted with Habib Tengour as to a possible English title for this Reader, he immediately suggested the phrase "Exile is my trade"?

Tengour has always written in French, and is of that generation for whom French was the closest language besides the mother-tongue, i.e. spoken Algerian Arabic. Skeptical in relation to the cultural claims of post-independence Algeria — especially those that would try to impose classical Arabic as the "real" or "original" language of a country where a dialectical variation of Arabic came to overlay several strong autochthonous Berber languages and the generalized use of the colonial imposition, French — Tengour would side with the great Algerian writer Kateb Yacine's claim that Arabic was just another, older colonial imposition, and that the Algerians had every right to keep French as the victor's war booty. In "'Postcolonial' Narrative and Identity: from *Ordeal by Bow* to *Moses' Fish*," one of the essays included in this book, Tengour writes about these matters, insisting that the language question is the wrong way of addressing problems of national or personal identity:

> I belong to the generation of the Tahar Djaout, Rachid Mimouni, Rabah Belrami, Abdelhamid Laghouati, Youcef Sebti, poets primarily. We did not escape the questioning about identity that tore the country apart. We dealt with it by refusing confinement inside the "false debate" around language, without however occulting the question of language. We all had learned French in school, we used it in our scriptural activities. In everyday orality, each one of us practiced his dialectical speech. I will not elaborate on this given fact, which we lived more or less badly….

French was our *spoils of war,* dearly paid for. To fall silent or to continue writing while knowing that the future would belong to the Arab language? Who could foresee the future? Nobody wanted to fall silent because identity and its narrative exceeded the imperatives of a political regime disconnected from the real. The political narrative is a discourse that veils the real; the poetical narrative is the real itself.

In the early essay "Langue, écriture et authenticité," he had already quoted Kateb Yacine on the question of the mother tongue, when he felt the need to focus more "crucially on the necessity for the writer to use the language of the people in order to touch the disinherited masses," rather than argue this language question on high cultural ground. Indeed, Kateb Yacine stopped writing in French (to devote himself to popular theater in spoken Algerian Arabic) after writing *Le polygone étoilé,* a book that ends with a reflection on the loss of the mother tongue, when Kateb the schoolboy, in love with his French schoolteacher, after making quick progress in learning the colonizer's language, is asked by his mother (jealous of the foreigner's language) to teach her French too:

> Never, even on those days of success with the school teacher, did I stop feeling deep down inside me this second rupture of the umbilical cord, this internal exile that brought the schoolboy closer to his mother only to tear them away, each time a little more, from the murmur of the blood, the reproachful shivering of a language banished, in a secret agreement broken as soon as made... Thus I had lost at the same time my mother and her tongue, the only inalienable — and yet alienated — treasures!

And Tengour sees this double pull as an inevitable, inescapable dialectic, commenting that "writing, no matter the language used, is never the language 'of the mother,' but always that of the 'teacher.'" A mother tells the tale that perpetuates the oral tradition yet very soon the school — and the wider social world beyond family or even tribe, especially in a modern urban setting — will take over. Through long effective training, one's language is socialized and a new imprint is made on mind and psyche. Later, of course, Tengour would argue, "the writer will have to reinvent an incantatory spontaneity from inside the servitude of the learned words." Cultural richness and literary complexity will in fact only arise from such (and other, further) mixings, multiplications, mestizo-ings. There is no such thing as a simple identity — whatever its ideological p.r. from those in power — be that in the Maghrib, in Europe or here in North America, the true *maghrib al-aqsa,* literally, the Far West.

Thus even if the quest for an Algerian identity is all-pervasive, the man and the writing are wiser than to think that such an identity can actually be achieved once or for all — or that it is more than just a fiction the heavy hand of the state wants to create in order to sedentarize the natural nomadism of man and poet. Tengour is clear about this, and if returns to Algeria are inscribed in the work again and again, just as they are in the writer's life, the space invoked in the work and actually lived-in belongs to a much wider and more shifting geography: the whole of the Mediterranean basin, the sea itself and its shores, the islands and the hinterland. Despite all the North-South p.r., the Mediterranean basin is a more culturally coherent area than first sight or first thought would permit one to believe. It would be useful in this context to reread the work of the French anthropologist, Germaine Tillion who called one of her books *Le Harem et les Cousins* (translated as *My Cousin, My Husband*) and showed how any inhabitant of the Mediterranean periplos — the area she called "the republic of the cousins," reaching from the Straits of Gibraltar to the Turkish coasts via El al-Djazā'ir, Mallorca & Marseilles, the Greek Islands & the Gulf of Tripoli — had more in common with each other than with any man or woman more than one hundred miles inland — north or south of there. Though of course, Tengour will go inland, as far as he can — or at least until he meets people who can't tell an oar from a winnowing tool.

This last image, borrowed from that core text of the Mediterranean periplos, *The Odyssey,* is not chosen by chance: if any figure is central to Tengour's work, it is that of Odysseus, or Ulysses. Thus his very first book, the poetic narrative *Tapapakitaques* (a neologism in which you can hear resound immediately the father and the island of Ithaca) opens with the line (which is thus also the first line of Tengour's published opus):

My name is ULYSSES I am twenty-two I study sociol-
ogy because I flunked law (p.9)

This identification continues throughout the later books — or is at least one of the personas Tengour inhabits. Though the figure is always already double: Ulysses is the twenty-two-year-old sociology student, but also the father figure and the king of his island. In a later essay, the author will have this to say concerning the Greek hero:

> Ulysses is king of Ithaca. He is the son of Laertes, the father of Telemachus, the husband of Penelope — he knows who he is, from where he comes; he keeps saying it and reminding himself of it in moments of captivity. At the same time, Ulysses is *Nobody*, which allows him to adopt all the personas necessary for his ruses in order to get out of trouble unscathed, without ever losing face, or at least that is what he believes. He divulges his name, which he states with pride and even arrogance, only once danger has been averted. His temerity induces him to brandish the signs that could identify him in front of those he loves. Yet his prudence envelops them in fictitious stories. To proceed masked, to scramble all the threads of the narrative while simultaneously desiring to be recognized immediately in all the facets of his identity, is what makes Ulysses suffer and he will be healed only by putting his "good oar" on his shoulder again, once he has overcome the ordeal of the bow.

Jacqueline Arnaud, in her essay "Ulysse et Sindbad dans l'imaginaire maghrébin," suggests that "turned upside down, desacralized, the terms of the myth allow Tengour to broach the Algerian themes, exile, the taking of power, the role of the poet, the revolution, in a displaced manner that disrupts the generally accepted ideas." The play on this Mediterranean tale is all the more effective as the geographical reference to Ithaca as an island rhymes with the Arabic name for Algeria, al-Djazā'ir, which translates literally as "the islands."

2.

One could call Tengour's poetics a "nomadic poetics," in reference both to the/his present condition of modern nomadicity between countries and languages, and to the nomadic Beduin ancestry of his culture and the ensuing influence of pre-Islamic poetry on his work, as detailed later, though one can also refer to it as an "archipelago poetics of relation" in reference to Edouard Glissant's theorizing of a (Caribbean) island poetics. At any rate, its core achievement is the successful relay between modernist Euro-American experiments and local traditions of sociopolitical and spiritual narrative explorations, or as he puts it toward the end of the "Maghribi Surrealism" essay: "It is, finally, in Maghribi Sufism that surrealist subversion inserts itself: 'pure psychic automatism,' *amour fou,* revolt, unexpected encounters, etc… There always resides a spark of un(?)conscious Sufism in those Maghribi writers who are not simply smart operators — go reread Kateb or Khaïr-Eddine."

Tengour's main books — besides the volumes of poetry to which we will come a bit later, the collection of short stories entitled *Gens de Mosta* (1997) and the novel *Le Poisson de Moïse* (2001) — are the prose narratives *Sultan Galiev* (1985) and *L'Epreuve de l'arc* (1990), a cycle started with *Le Vieux de la Montagne* (1983). Aware of the question of genre definition, he succeeded in side-stepping the French cartesian (and commercially motivated?) preference for calling any text that is, or looks like prose, a "roman," i.e. novel, by calling his cycle a "Relation." The choice of this term is not innocent. The French word "relation" (as does its Spanish homonym) names a genre: that of the travelogue. But this French word (and genre) is immediately ghosted by its Arabic equivalent: the *riḥla*. A word that derives, as Pandolfo tells us, "from the verbal root *raḥla*, to set out, to depart, to move away, to emigrate, to be constantly on the go, to wander, to lead a nomadic life." The noun, meaning travel, is also the name of the genre of the travelogue, "a classical literary genre of travel writing which blossomed in Dār al-Islam, the 'land of Islam,' from the eleventh to the fifteenth century and lasted in different forms all the way to the nineteenth century." Its origins are in the diaristic writings describing an individual's hajj, or journey to Mecca, though it expanded rapidly to take in other kinds of travels, and was in fact a place of literary innovation. Pandolfo further explicates its importance:

> The *riḥla* as physical journey and existential displacement was the style and possibility of learning. Across the Islamic world, from one center of learning to another, a constant flow of scholars moved on endless peregrinations: from teacher to teacher, and from text to text… the imperative

of traveling for seeking knowledge determined the cosmopolitan character of the centers of learning, where everyone was a foreigner and everyone belonged.

One further aspect of this genre is useful for us here:

> The *riḥla* is also a philosophical genre of narratives of displacement. It is a genre that might be called "cynical." As is the case of the Maqāmāt discussed by Kilito… it is a narrative genre of reflections about the journey-like character of life, the instability of fate and of the world, the irony of human existence and what Kilito names "l'identité fugitive" [fugitive identity], in the context of a "celebration of instability." (316)

Le Vieux de la Montagne, published in 1983, and the two subsequent volumes of the cycle, are a tour-de-force text that re-inscribes the genre of the *riḥla,* and its diasporic intensities, into a contemporary context of nomadic movement, both in time and place, as well as in its language and poetics. The first volume thus re-imagines through contemporary Maghribi characters in their Occidental exile in Paris, the story of that most famous Mashreqi Arab triumvirate of Omar Khayyam, Hassan as-Sabbah, and Nizam al-Mulk. Just as Abdelwahab Meddeb breaks the transhumance (not a true nomadicity) between that "unwobbling pivot" that for so many Maghribi writers is the Algiers/Casablanca/Tunis – Paris axis, (the umbilical cord that links the ex-colony to the old "metropole" and its language) by having his writing move through the Mashriq, i.e. the eastern parts of the Arab countries, especially Egypt and Ibn Arabi's Damascus, so Tengour re-nomadizes, re-diasporises his work by moving through those classic loci of Arab culture in the Nippur and Baghdad of the tenth to twelfth centuries. This is not cultural tourism, but a necessary re-appropriation to break free of the aforementioned axis. Nor is it a nostalgic rear-view mirror recollection of the long-gone glory of classical Arab civilization at the height of its powers. For to work with and through those specific figures, emigrating their ghosts into the fictional bodies of present-day Maghribis in Western exile, also has to be read in terms of a poetics — or even of a poethics, to use Joan Retallack's word. If we can locate the birth of an urban, modernist Western poetics, with all the experimental and avant-gardist baggage this entails, in the late nineteenth century with Whitman in Europe, and Baudelaire and Rimbaud in France (no doubt an oversimplification, but a useful shorthand nonetheless), and still use those achievements as paradigmatic for our current endeavors, then, when looking at the Arab world we will have to widen our horizons beyond our chronology.

To understand not only the surface diasporicity of this endeavor, but to get to a deeper sense of the poetics — and their transformations — underlying these writings, including their genre classifications, we need a brief excursus into the history of Arabic poetics. For, as the Syrian poet Adonis has shown, just such a breakthrough had happened in urban Baghdad a millennium and more ago when poets like Abu Nuwas broke with the traditional, classical Arab poetics, whose origins go back to the pre-Islamic *Mu'allaqat* (Odes) which served as fixed and by then sterile molds — both in terms of form and content — for poetry. Claiming the past modernity of Arab poetics via those figures also claims and reclaims a non-religiously based ethics, today, in the face of a return, desired or imposed, to a puritanical Islam that would burn exactly this old/modern part of its own avant-garde heritage: the wine-drinking, boy-loving Baghdadi poets who broke the sterile molds of inherited forms and wrote the first works in which we can recognize the shapes of our own experimental modernities.

But let us take a closer look at one of Tengour's poems from the 1980s, "Les Sandales d'Empédocle," first published in Michel Deguy's magazine *Po&sie,* and in my English translation as a chapbook from Duration Press in 1999. It presents itself *ab initio* in an astoundingly wide nomadicity: the author's name clearly locates him as an Arab, while the title refers to a Greek philosopher situated in Italy, and the epigraph cites a nineteenth-century German poet, Friedrich Hölderlin. There is Poundian or post-Poundian modernity visibly at work here, confirmed by the poem itself, which reads as a modernist textual montage/collage of a wide-ranging array mixing the personal & the historical. The opening lines set the tone of contemporaneity, down to the slashes used to separate the word-shards:

Traces/ Renown/ Shades/ Urns/ Life(s)/ Epoch/ Zenith/ Lucid/ Strangely/ Suspended

The thirteen-page text itself gives one — or at least this reader — the familiar sense of late-twentieth-century open-field poetics, as collaged elements move through space and time, interrupting and questioning the possibilities of the micro-narratives that develop from time to time, creating momentary pools of meditative or contemplative loci often reflecting on the act of writing itself, before dissolving as quickly as they appear. The concerns are nearly classical diasporic moves between urban centers, questions of exile, of racial identity, of the political situation in the unnamed Maghribi country that is clearly Algeria, the matter of love under such circumstances — an urban, post-*Waste Land* land and psycho-space. To this extent, Tengour's poem is a work that, besides the usual questions of tone and pitch, is rather exhilarating for a translator putting it into contemporary English. But a close reading reveals that this poem too is ghosted by the consciously worked absence/presence of a formal skeleton that links it directly to an ancient genre of Arab poetry: the ode or *qasida*.

A brief excursus is necessary here. The qasida represents the earliest extent Bedouin Arab poetry, the purest examples of which are the seven — in some canonic calculations, ten — pre-Islamic Mu'allaqat, often called the "Hanging Poems" (because, embroidered on lengths of cloth, they used to be hung from the Ka'aba, the black stone in Mecca, on festive occasions). They are often described as stilted, overdetermined, static poems because of their supposedly predetermined closed structures and monorhymes. Of greatly varying length, the odes usually start in the same place, the atlāl, or meditation on the traces of an old camp the poet comes across in his wanderings. A. Hamori, cited by Pandolfo, writes in his *The Art of Medieval Arabic Literature*:

> It can be safely said that the atlāl motif is the most dramatic among the various nasīb-themes [introductory section of the qasida] — such as the description of parting, or a dream-visit by the lady's phantom — in that it contrasts the irreversible time of human experience with the recurrences possible in nature... In the atlāl scene time present has no effective contents to speak of. The past has a specific burden; the present is indeterminate except by reference to a memory. The speaker arrives at a desolate

but familiar spot; we are not told what business led him there... in this way the emptiness at the conclusion of the affair is given a depth of time... The atlāl are the point where the temporal and spatial coordinates meet.

After this introduction the poem continues with a hymn to the poet's mount, camel or horse, (thus a moment of stasis followed by precipitous movement) after which it will often laud the poet's lady, then his weapons and exploits in the manner of the praise poem, before going on to tell of the tribe's great feats. What is fascinating, even or especially for our contemporary poetics, is the rhizomatic way in which the poem, inside that set structure, proceeds via series of images, moving from realm to realm, human — animal — vegetable — mineral, and back up, away & around & through, horizontal & vertical, taproots, transfers, without the felt need for a fixed or "organic" development. Writes Jacques Berque:

This process, where one or the other series alternate, does not worry about coherency. Its most moving aspect, I mean its most mobilizing aspect, is the heteroclite richness of its calls [appels], much more so than their respective compatibility or their mutual cohesion. What is important for this process is, literally, to *transfer*. It takes the trope seriously, or at least has not yet had the time to reduce it exclusively to a rhetoric. And that rhetoric is also present in some of these poems, permitting the outrageous, the ironic and the precious to come through, as well as the reflexive from the instinctive, the factive from the originary, — it is that *dérive*, no, that perpetual hunt from realm to realm, from stadium to stadium, from genre to genre, that could appear as specifically Arabic. [my translation]

What the poet's role can be, today in the ongoing oral tradition that still makes use of this form, or of variations thereof, is brilliantly analyzed by Stefania Pandolfo in the chapter "Impasse of the Angels" in the book of that title. In a footnote she cites Abdelfattah Kilito, who calls the poet a "melancholic archeologist" — an appellation I cannot help but link to Charles Olson's description of the poet as "archeologist of morning" —

whose job is "to draw over a drawing, to write over a text half-effaced. Confronted with writing in time the poet must add something of his own for a new settlement to be born" [Pandolfo's translation].

With this in mind we can now return to Tengour's poem — and it immediately becomes obvious that the very title, despite its displacement into Greco-Italian areas, in itself sets the scene of an abandoned site where only ruins — the abandoned sandals — remain to speak of a past human presence. The epigraph inserted between title and poem insists again on just this situation, even if once more or further displaced by being in German. Hölderlin's lines — re-cited in French translation late in the poem itself — read:

> this country where the purple grape once loved
> to grow for a better people, and the golden fruit
> in the dark thicket, and noble wheat, and some day
> the stranger will ask, treading through the rubble
> of your temples, if this is where the city
> rose...?

Through his diasporic knowledge, the poet is able to read this poem fragment firmly rooted in German romanticism, as another version of the classical Arabic atlāl motif, the stopping (here of a stranger, not the poet) at the ruins. And, as if Tengour wanted to nail this theme down, despite his wandering through other spatial-temporal realms in title and epigraph, the very first word of the poem, after the already-cited, slash-separated words, and given a line by itself, is "Stop." A "stop" modulated in the next line as "a pause of short duration," which, knowing what we know now, we can read not only as the hasty modern nomadic traveler's brief respite (in "one-night cheap hotels"), but further as the Arabic "mawqif" — a term used, among others, by the tenth-century Sufi poet Niffari and meaning the pause, the stop-over, the rest, the stay of the wanderer between two moments of movement, two runs, two sites, two places, two states. Abdelwahab Meddeb comments on this mawqif: "It enjoys a rest, raises itself upright; between two durations it scrutinizes briefly the instant when from its height it confronts the vision or the word exteriorizing itself." It is the space/time in which the poem will happen, where the poet can get to work. If we now turn back to those slash-separated words between epitaph and body of the text, we can read these differently too:

"Traces/ Renown/ Shades/ Urns/ Life(s)/ Epoch/ Zenith/ Lucid/ Strangely/ Suspended" now reveal themselves to be not only a modernist collage of fragments but descriptions of the different sections of the poem, here adhering to the old qasida structure, here departing from it as seems necessary to the poet in order to shape that old formal ghost to his, and his world's, contemporary needs and realities.

The whole of the poem can now be read at a much more complex level than a first straightforward reading of its surface contemporaneity allows. This analysis of one of Tengour's poems, if not applicable directly to all of the work, does however indicate the thematic and formal complexities of the writing — a complexity that not surprisingly is just as present in his prose narratives. If, as shown above, modernist collage techniques are essential in structuring the various heterogenous elements of the Tengourian universe in a poem such as the "Sandal of Empedocles," then related techniques are demonstrably used in the narratives. Concerning these one could speak of an amalgam as savant as it is witty of writing drawing on oral traditions from the Maghrib transformed for contemporary writerly purposes and leavened by cinematic montage — via Tengour's fascination with, love for, and knowledge of the one new twentieth-century art form: film. A love that is obvious in the writing itself as film often enters both as formal procedure and thematic process. Thus, if as already indicated, Odysseus is an archetypal figure of the Tengourian imagination, this archetype must not be understood as a backwards pointing fixity, but as a multi-faceted cubist construction, or, better, a fluid Eisensteinian montage of shimmering facets: one facet will propose the Homeric/Mediterranean prototype, the next one may call on the emblematically modernist figure of the Joycean Ulysses on a pub-crawl, though a quick *fondu-enchaîné* will complicate the dance by introducing the Hollywoodian antics of Kirk Douglas' Ulysses tangling with Silvana Mangano — who in a further de-doubling happens to play both Circe and Penelope in that 1953 movie that could be seen as a core event in a young Tengour's discovery of the world!

This is not the place for a lengthy critical analysis of the work, but, before closing the introduction to let Tengour's work speak for itself, I would like to briefly address the question of translation or translatability. Is this "ghost" of Arabic I have shown to haunt the French text, translatable, or better, is it necessary for the translator to try and foreground it? In the "Sandal," the poet himself has half-buried the old qasida form in his poem — as if this form itself was the ruin at which he stops, so that the "melancholic archeologist" can be seen to meditate as much on the ruins of the old form as on the questions of contemporary diasporic life. The two situations overlap, covering and enriching each other: isn't the chance discovery of an old site also the contemporary experience of today's diasporic wanderer? The poem is thus itself already a translation, i.e. a diasporic construct — Tengour's diasporic French ghosted by an old Arab nomad form, playfully deepening the absence/presence through the Greco-Italian-German layers. It seems to me that — and I believe this to be true in most cases — a translation should be as literal as possible, that is to say, it should adhere to the same absence/presence structure the poem uses. The poem's "ghost" is as invisible to the reader of the original French version as it is to the reader of the English version — unless the reader already has knowledge of those old Arabic forms. Otherwise the reader, French or English, will have to do an in-depth reading of the poem, which for any such diasporic writing means familiarizing oneself with the other's other culture. A translation should not, cannot make clearer what the original poem has purposefully hidden.

I have approached the rest of the translations in this book in the same spirit, no matter the genre — poem or prose — of the original. Though a good part of the translation work was done during a concentrated period in the summer of 2010, the earliest attempts and versions date back some twenty years at least, given that my interest in Tengour's work goes back a very long time indeed — to the days we taught together at the University of Constantine, Algeria in the late seventies. I have had the great pleasure of being in continuous touch with the man and his work ever since and thus believe that my familiarity with the development of the *oeuvre* can only have helped the work of translation gathered here for the first time.

Pierre Joris, Bay Ridge, January/February 2011

Resources:

Jacqueline Arnaud, "Ulysse et Sindbad dans l'imaginaire maghrébin," pp. 536–553 in *L'homme méditerranéen et la mer : actes du Troisième Congrès international d'études des cultures de la Méditerranée Occidentale*, Jerba, Avril 1981 / publié par Micheline Galley et Leïla Ladjimi Sebai. Imprint Tunis : Les Editions Salammbé, c1985.

Abdelkebir Khatibi, *Love in Two Languages*, translation by Richard Howard, University of Minnesota Press, 1990.

Abdelfattah Kilito, *Les séances: récits et codes culturels chez Hamadhanî et Harîrî*, Paris, Sindbad, 1983.

Stefania Pandolfo, "The Thin Line of Modernity in some Moroccan Debates on Subjectivity" in *Questions of Modernity*, eds. T. Mitchell and L. Abu-Lughod. The University of Minnesota Press, 2000.

Ulysses (1955) Film based on Homer's *Odyssey*. Directed by Mario Camerini, who co-wrote the screenplay with writer Franco Brusati. With Silvana Mangano (Circe & Penelope); Kirk Douglas (Odysseus); Anthony Quinn (Antinous).

POETRY

From *The Arc and the Scar*

CAFÉ MARINE (LETTERS)

Constantine, 1 January 1978

The dream is red that rams the ebony of desire in the evening misunderstanding (why are the keys dirty I soliloquized in the cold of my feet with the sun of January First to caress the bareness of the hunt we must have lost ourselves when we opened the door to become you no longer recognized the things that offered themselves so I'll explain myself

Ulysses is an old movie with Silvana Mangano (emotion) Kirk Douglas and Anthony Quinn. Unfortunately Penelope was not in *Gunfight at O.K. Corral.* That's culture for you. Our childhood was beautiful because we survived it.

As far as the tale is concerned, the gaze does not always spread.

I am writing you these few lines to give you some of our news; we are in good and perfect health and hope it is so for you too.

....

It rained when Ulysses landed in Ithaca.
Alone on the shingle beach, he grabbed a pebble and beat his head
repeatedly. An adolescent who was bathing nearby came up to him.

Something wrong, mister?
No, thanks... My head's a bit heavy
Ah!

He walked up to the Palace.

Homer will say that nobody recognized him, except the old dog. But
dogs don't live long enough to recognize their masters.

It was a holiday and he was allowed in to beg a piece of bread. Only
one of the Suitors spoke to him   nicely
it was not the youngest among them   but he knew himself to be lost
among all the others.

The beggar advised him to leave the place   which
he took as an insult. But the stranger made such an impression on him
that he was able to escape the massacre.

In Ithaca many things are told concerning this famous day and the Trial
of the Bow.
But Ulysses had simply said: everybody out, this is my Home!

The Suitors were   ...   by the situation.
The beggar had been energetic but that hadn't created an uproar. The
Suitors were tired from their wait and
                                        Curious
about this newcomer.
What if it really was Ulysses come back to Ithaca?!
That'd be a riot, and they wanted to know what would happen.

(weren't the designs of the gods unfathomable)

Let's split said Antinoüs: if it is Ulysses we
got it coming.

Penelope didn't recognize him   she who
Said   you've been a long time coming sweetheart
Ulysses stripped burned his rags and wept into
the flame.

What are you looking for? the companions ask
                 can't you see pain invading
our dreams…
, the saliva has a bitter taste like the past spells
the call of pumice stones the caress haunts
Time to go home
She who holds the sailor *of a thousand triCks*
hauntIng
erR
plaCated body/the Journey
strangE like the Return   patiently

Ulysses had left in order to test Absence and after having killed his
companions, he wound up in a vacant lot.

Dawn revealed the dream glum with dew

When he woke to love she had gone beyond the burn in hand

and scoffed at him with her sad smile.

But did she even look at him? You are dead she had said and if you
make love to me I'll be sleeping with a corpse; now nothing can happen
to me anymore.

(Much later he'll understand what she said and the island's immobile
blue that irritated his companions enough to leave him.)

Goats scoured the garbage dump.

The shepherd who saw the drifter lying there on the ground offered him
a cigarette and turned on his transistor
blaring the news of the world…

Many had died for an *empty tunic* and exile dispersed us. Ulysses found
an old woman bent over her loom, indifferent...   The
bitterness of the days,
tirelessly.
Of all the warriors
                ?
Just a tiff between neighbors
and Shades Ulysses vainly wanted to pierce!

Calypso carried the heavy scent
Of all the seas crossed
                    and the sailor watched as she deloused her dreams

Why bring up what were days of nostalgia?

Ulysses was God for her Her who was weeping over forgotten
Garlands

One day the seashell told him the immortality of an odyssey
he asked to go home

It's in the No Future bar that Ulysses gets his companions to commit to the break heavy with desire.

He orders the first round and they drank until closing time. They woke up bitter days at the tragic weaving of the tale where daily enchantment
                         reveals itself
useless at grasping the innate melancholy of circles.

          At the helm
                    Ulysses
                         exhorted
                              the crew
          to ballast their dreams to the hazardous blue

(to have done with the servitude of breakfast)

I'll gratify your gaze Ulysses tells his Companions and you'll see

we'll bend down the moon to polish the lips' trembling with
the wonder of lavender honey

and the childish spectacle of discoveries to be re-named
in our fingers' salty noon

Far from the hurt that hollows the gaze nimble at connecting
Far from dying...
What to expect from the Journey the Companions ask

And twenty years later Ulysses came home alone. He went straight
to the CAFÉ DE LA MARINE and after paying
for drinks all around,

I'll gratify your gaze, he says...

The street in a coat of tamed otter-skin
I love you she said

Not even an echo
The pint of beer empty without liking beer

Evenings a muted gaze

Did she know how he loved her

He pronounced her name in a jam-packed
brasserie where nobody took heed of him.

Will she wait for him?

He bit a trembling hand   saw
again her wet smile   And

...........................my darling,
Ulysses dreamed the fragility of the trembling foam
        murmur of the days

consumed
An Iliad in the pyre of the toothless hired mourners

The Companions were wise to prefer olive oil to the trade of adventurer

                            ...

Ithaca in the swelling of the chests but Ulysses' eloquence was
disturbing in its images

Rousing

And each one to die in the turmoil of their dew-swollen skins

She was in front of him the substitute as echo
He was sailor in the curvature of desire
(we met so as to burn our gazes)

She took his breath in a sleep drenched dawn
He interrogated her body in the despair of ports of call
(we tore ourselves to bits to meet our dreams)

The Companions grunted under the stick
They groaned the nostalgia of dried mud houses

... don't leave yet

He found timid shadows in the secret of the evocation

She said stay in the beauty of my language
We woke up

He said am I still Ulysses
it's been awhile I'm trying to get back
home where my wife waits for me my son and my dog too
perhaps my father too and my good old wet nurse
all of them
over there on Ithaca
languishing for me

She   beloved mortal
aren't you happy to invest my bed
to taste each moment that passes the return
to the same
just as a god does
an immortality your dead
companions would envy you

He says I've aged despite my appearance
I no longer bathe with the same pleasure
It happens that I forget my kin it only lasts
the time of a sigh already I torment myself
isn't it strange that I am here talking to you

She my poor love
what strange torment do you suffer in silence
do you believe I chain you like a miserable
docile dog to my passing whim
of wind then leave
I am divine but a woman and I love to be beseeched

He says I love you but it's not easy for me

She doesn't answer

So far away   that that isn't the place
counters images   they become rare

Light smile thus at the dawn of the encounter

indecisive as in the past

Sailor who dreams among his bottles
of the siren of the headland

THATCH, WATER-MEADOW AND SHEET METAL

Autumn

> *I'll go over there where the tree and man...*
> —Charles Baudelaire

Grooves calcinated remains
Dwelling emptied of dreams
You exhausted the gaze of all the designated spaces
To die the path

Like the rope gone to earth
Like the gallop that has lost its cadence
Like the boldness of dawn

Where the feared halt — oblivion of first steps

How many lulls in our lives
Over there a vine dries in the white sun
Over there my body had shattered on the ground
So much desire in the well-loved lull

...
The days imagine the sand deserted
Parade

Love me, oh...
Pain, bodies toiling at the incidence of remorse
(How not to die for having bathed my heart in
your body)
Dream torn from the well-established fear

Oh love me
The signs fade away one after the other and lose themselves in silence

And you, unsettled, what do you expect from silence...

Offered myrrh
Scepter laid down to the day that rises naked
Trembling encounter

Our lives crossed to lose themselves forever
To weep over the place today, mutilated memory
The pain masters the words

You present yourself with a patched up story
A soul yellowed by time
What hope do you hold in the words gone awry

As evening closed in I heard the tears
And our lives looked at each other

For a long time the wound suspended like a reprimand
…

Building site
Long ago a man lost his hands
Freed from the embrace's whiteness

From early morning on the noise confounds all the signs
Wake-up is tough

An image persists that wants to dominate your life
Subdue the shadow of the song

You turn moved because the sun is already high

Marbled heights
You contemplate sunset at the close of a crisis
Mirror with no resonance
Destitution of effects
Your life collides with the other shore — your mortgaged soul

You say I didn't want that/my face
And you say Fate under the mask
A snatched promise

She
Worried
Looks at you and looks and looks

(Look at yourself!)

...

at the close of a crisis mirror with no resonance

...

to Kh.

Somber signs knotted into the deep solid ochre
Pain, light   quartered — rejection of brightness
Headway in the insomnia shell
The azure/marine dream drowns the expected color

That's my way of traveling he said

From: *The Gravity of the Angel*

THE RAFT OF MEMORY

... taking a well-balanced oar, you must set forth
until you come to men
who do not know the sea
nor ships with purple prows
nor balanced oars
that are a ship's wings
and take no salt in their food.
... when another sojourner, having fallen in with you,
says that you carry a winnowing fan
on your illustrious shoulders,
then stick your balanced oar into the earth
and make a handsome offering to Lord Poseidon:
ram, bull, and wild boar that mounts sows...

Odyssey, XI — transl. by Charles Stein

Shore
on the dampened sand you survey
light and salt   — drowsy

you smile
to what surrounds you older you present yourself
on the island in the silence

the sea proposes no complicity and you bathe
alone in an evocation said to be innocent

the long voyage faraway derisory
The art of accosting forgotten
all reference points muddled up

from shore to scar a gaze's intention slides

Ulysses' palace the amnesiac isle
kids clusters of shellfish
chiseled coral
vendor with settled breath

far the school the gardens

it hurts

more than wounded salt
more than sea-obscure

you tell Ulysses's tale a kid
marveling a proffered sponge

a soul to be invested
what profits suggests the revived talk
insignificant

The fly is white bee with wings deployed
the master says dizzy from scientific assurance
of parceled purity in the marine world
it sanctifies the fauna intrigues the visitor
it dips the mosaic into the strange dailyness

penetration in the tableau transported
enigma by the voice powerful majestic
theatricality of an augural decor

image, manner
inextinguishable suite inexpressible received

the schoolboy sees no bee in the waves
but notices an octopus happy to scoff at him

the hurled nets immobile contemplation

Lookout at the summit
and the sea sitting
suspension of a weft

the island desert since
black scorpions heavy with poisons vipers
brackish water bouncer of sailors
micaceous sand shimmers a murky blue-green

stones heaped in the north wind

the entrusted promise is there
heedful of the visitor's beating

She naked cleaving the water in nascent dawn
immobile mirror dilated
in exaltation recognition of the hours
spent sumptuous and transparent and blessed

a lie peacock ostrich
a weft weighed down with remorse
a fissure you observe growing wider
seizing your blood in plenary session

passion for patched up pieces
affable then numbed
lapidary hearth

the sea disgorged us of corrupt wisdom
on a shore of tarred algae naked as in a dream
& blue dawn of fog still lingers on our lips

A star a vase
and what is the string that hides the irradiated soul
jubilant passenger
— this fear of stumbling

on fire in sweat
audacity of a pause
keep me in the lamp
already the star hurls the first blade

meditating
a leaning to capture
aroma of a wave rich night coming undone

you grow pale god in the breeze and plumb me
idyl to become knife
morning clearing of rocks

Suddenly nothing and you reappear
and command to relive beyond

so many words draped in ermine
the taciturnity of a night bird
the garment torn by simple atavism

toward the isle by chance temporary accommodation
captive and the sailboard
to leave home nearly dead to die
alone
and go on
there on the island as if nothing had happened
you return to demand the ransom of a vision
to destroy a soul devastated by its journeys

you are my domain my link I settle in at home
and deliver you for I have learned to behave myself

Innocently those over there come to you
perilous summons you scramble the fire
words to be auctioned off
and the freshly minted stubborn instant gives in

I know who you are
you are the inviting gaze and torment
my most beautiful image still untamed
raised in front of the altar

whirlwind he worries
night futile to reassure an encounter

you say I am deserted by tenderness
answer: forgive my breathless hands

for a long time this distress denies itself my lips

On that day
we will raise up our lives wine unmixed united
in the crystal
a sign wakes up

For a long time
fixation of a timbre, any vanishing trace
sprayed
   — conjuration —
you said you were mourning me today

One threshold and it's exile
there's only easy temptation
           too much! of a sob
a decision put off to later
        overzealous preparations
flow into the vise you gasp for breath, at times.

...
You say you surprise me without knowing it half-way to a dream
to set traps for her who is delayed you in fact

What to do
as your ruses draw close
       you induce the night to blush
a dusty turmoil
      love me in the light

Our bodies wrangle our stranded lives sea-urchin
shells

Inspire me, she says, now that I caught you.

SHALES OF TAHMAD 2

I think of whoever has lost what can never be found again.
—Charles Baudelaire

    window   feast
    inclines the gaze

    she says: tear me away

    liberates a night
    goes out

    enamored

Porte d'Aix
family smell
the bus passes
love stuck to the window

season of exile

regulated entry
austere sense
a craziness

state police troopers...

there are dark passions
a chant that transpires
the people come and go

as the storm nears
are we

of an arrogance
to walk a scarlet semblance
legacy
with sequences of sands

to support a capital punishment
in the profusion
slowly
day goes astray

an Arab veiled in locusts
urges on his mare struts
about and hums
begs for applause

he his kin know the toll
two dinars a head the Occident

I recognize him
she says strip him

of all his goods keep only a ram
offer it to the one who no longer waits

Djaziya commanded the men
knew how to handle the epigram
she from a high linage and expert
was going to submit
...
and Dhiyâb the hilalian marries Djaziya

It is only a story
to lull a fever
words like a vault
consigned with sadness
to nothing our traces
the salt in the cinders
in   ecstasy

Place, a blade's indecision
against the grain awakening

our giddiness a screen
was it a need to parade

iridescent, with abrasive points
gashes sulfur the trace

in its crack blue from freezing
at the hour when winter cards the park

the bird asks to drink at night
your blood cracks like bark

Lotus as tattoo
opulence of haymaking times
there crushed by insolence

this memory shakes you up
you say inadvertently
let them guess

invariably you slide into invective
friable shell — rendezvous of insects
you heart goes away

late lightnesses

murderous clay
night kneads then rejects
contour in suspension

Showers
the dream pulls back
the charms no longer work metal
alone
slices
corruption
knacker's work… CENSORSHIP

night takes ahold of the course
a hand forgets the loved one's dictation
panic

dawn mechanically scalds the gaze
opens the scared crystal
heady facets

shines a solid pain
so much

at the point of dawn
the promises went by

passion interior of a wall
consumed in the instant
gaping

dare break
throw yourself at my sweat
let your fears regale themselves on my flesh
I reserve you an exile in my equipage

departure
to wish to die

dew

a bracelet gone astray
              enthralls you

in the hip swaying day
              idol

with surprise worn off
              the obol dazzles the corpse

cheap junk aggresses the sidewalks
              fired clay shatters

laud this ordeal
              far from the sunset's wrinkles

the coffee smoking   gold
zinc   mornings

train of saucers
shroud

red than ochre than smokey
in the silence of a set up
happy
the town is drying up

summer encloses
lesion here
fusion of alum — sortilege

to see again the refused threshold
to understand

in the turmoil
one despairs
the bodies sway
din
a memory still

the heatwave's rust overwhelms
stealthily
this celebrated speech
performer of cements   dead

(a dog licked the moon
in the middle of mute ruins)

where are you night revelers
there
you dive into
sleep
a rupture to be transmitted

from *The State of Things* followed by *Hodgepodge*

FIVE MOVEMENTS OF THE SOUL
(first version)

Gray in
soul
this voice

goes to earth
report &
worried it

laments
oh
has sung

has taken
friend
body of evocation

In silence
soul at
at the threshold

at a loss
awaiting
then stretching

stone dream
river
a door

clear
has smiled
it did not last

Rumors
soul twists in the
dark

its voice loses itself
amphitheater
empty

flow
saccade
this soft listening

there where
no meeting
is visible

Return
refinds itself
the eye

soul's mirror
the other soul
at the tournament

to let go
instant
that fate fixes

as day breaks
both
exhaust themselves

This soul
at day's end
tautens

alone in
the store
its memory

shadow often
coldly
blames

right then turns
away from
you

HODGEPODGE

I.

At first sight, they are only incoherent games. Grotesque fillers. Show-off non-sense. Smacking of the platitudinous. Formal variations for the pleasure of an elite. An elixir! Today's reader is bored faced with the complexity of the techniques put into play. He understands nothing of all these sassy-smart experiments with language. The newspaper speaks differently to him. Each day a new catastrophe engulfs him in anguish. Blood all over the reported stories. A woof of unforeseeable elements where it is difficult to recognize the golden threads of the embroidery.

II.

The practiced constraint falsifies syntax. Intervals insinuate themselves into the distortion of the vocabulary. The narrative obeys no causality. Events follow each other without any change. This amuses some stylists who see in it an exemplary freedom. But such juggling is incapable of silencing the empty bellies. Everywhere one bumps into a dubious meaning. One looks for words with an edge to get the upper hand. In fact, the choices remain limited. The nouns prevail over the verbs and adjectives. Terrible toponyms. Chiseled obscenities. Irremediable blasphemies. Unhealthy scatologies. Repugnant names of animals or people. Earmarking of certain body parts. All of which teems in a triviality that provokes a slight disgust.

III.

It borders on a macabre polyphony. One doesn't listen to one another anymore in the middle of the tableau. There's something in it for everyone, he says. But it doesn't add up. It is not a question of a simple stroke of the pen. You see how heavy the slightest word weighs down on language. To ferret it out hasn't been a picnic. You suffer faced with the contradictions of the lexicon in the ever slighter hope of finding a way out. Language is never free or profuse despite signs of an opening up. It is a bleeding that can't be staunched. A local color lacking the emphasis of time.

Beyond that, an apparent emptiness produces an effect of contrast.

from *Traverser*

(....)

The sea. How did it thus become the sea?
Moire
and the words separate peddled in a morning's innocence.

A sure friend
if there is need for an assurance in friendship
poet
appeared in my dream
to warn me of the regrettable consequences to exoticism
that manifest themselves
                              imago
                                        here under the eye
                                                      amused over there
the Arabs are kitsch
truth is massaged it's unbearable
I've said that this has never stopped anyone from sleeping.
I was wrong.
In fact, I couldn't bear the sermonizers any longer
even in my sleep.
It's indecent!
But the time will come when writers will get together in plain daylight
and without any artifice
they'll dig up the mandrakes with bayonets
(the image becomes trivial after the state of siege, the curfew
and the assassinations).
The freedom to present publicly what undermines being
takes on meaning.
Shop windows shatter.
There isn't much to sell here.
Does that change the facts?

I had to hold my own in the mire momentarily
stir up much mud in the hope of finding a little water.
Whirlwinds in Heraclitus' wake.
To be sensible.
Correct manners, and that's enough!
Put an end to the all too sturdy transition.
Don't you find that you are dangerously drifting
away from your first fervors?
You wrap up the merchandise in full view of the tanks!...
The stale trash bags of the awakening flouted premonition.
Tasks...
All I wanted to see in the dream was a sequence of clichés.
Collective memory knew how to hide its bunkers under the cacti but its
archaic ruses cannot resist an attack made according to the rules.
Certain shores disillusion but the obsession continues under the mask.
I was always had.

A year finishes
it starts up again
. the ash there
hunts vagaries of desire
snowy grayness the dissimulations
an illusory everyday

global warming is abnormal
it perturbs the enclosed transparency of an ingenuous garden

The Garden of the Hesperides was delivered ready for immediate occu-
pancy after Heracles had tested it: therefore also it no longer provides
juicy exportable fruit as in the days of Massinissa who, despite the sordid
ways in which he is overlooked by history books, owes his living fame to
the literal application,
from A   to Z
        of an authentic scientifically conceived agrarian

revolution.
A challenge to the laws of the market. The souk.
Berber utopia…
Birth of a nation.
It was the time of trading posts and inshore navigation
but already
we were disemboweling each other for the conquest of markets
the convertible living space
of preventive wars
to deprive the other of any warlike desire
a rubbish heap by chance abandoned
fat foam laps at the feet of rusty
stones conjuring up the barter of olives of wheat
and the fantasy of the rhapsodes
who secretly among themselves were relaying the myth of
Aphrodite

The coastal sites were to begin with colonies founded by industrious wops escaping the perfidious gossip of their cities of birth. One was leaving the resonant Orient were speech was highly prized and graded to seek refuge in the Occident known to be barbarous. Barbarism was a relative state, a negotiable point of view. An imperial logic was developed based on accident of landing place. Or the virtue of the Lares gods. Or matrimonial strategies. The new goods quickly loosened the tongues. Search for eloquence. Treatises on style. The strongest was always right and if need be could always invoke the inalienable law of return. He knew how to impose his books and his culinary art. There remains as proof of this fossil wine in sealed amphoras sometimes fished up from the deep rubble of engulfed wharfs.
We arrived later along dromedary trails, which explains nothing. Two submerging waves. The second one was compared to a plague of locusts. We exchanged our habits under the newcomers' nose.
But this is not an explanation.

We is another hunchback I don't recognize when he prevents me from getting some fresh air or from singing in the moonlight. Settled on an island, when the fever seizes him as it does today on the public squares, he brutally ignores the call of the sea and diving, and woman escaped his shortsightedness.

This thing, woman, it does his head in!

The phenomenon is cyclical. It's all the rage.

Others have landed, inside the coordinates of the meridian of Greenwich (I learned that it passed close by Mostaganem, through the courtyard of the castle where Petrus Borel suffered a sunstroke),

loving cruises, boisterous rhythms and forbidden swimming.

They ate us up alive. Then regurgitated us.

After that, they took us, body and soul.

Sidi Lakhdar had warned us.

"Hokum — the cult of the saints is a perversion of the original religion." Belouahrani is said to even have predicted Aids and that secretly an Arab would find the vaccine. "They are only verses," they retort. "The vision of a distraught person. A dubious interpretation."

The fourteenth century!

It caused great pain. I no longer suffer.

They took care of my execution.

(...)

Dubious dawn
and sunrise sweats
with what hairy strength tone up one's soul
how to speak of love
logically to love with unabating
passion when there is no opportunity
another question awaits the young man
at the bus stop an enigma
after she had thrown herself from the top of the rock
space shrinks
the stars pass by before midnight
the sea riles the gaze
what blue
isn't it dictatorship
one repeats the question: isn't it **dictatorship**
you think twice
and don't answer
the perimeter knows
from experience the facets are multiple
and variable according to the fashions
the coral snake and the leech larvae and the corrupted seeds and the obtuse silence and ass licking and enflamed preaching and the bastard crew and the most knowledgeable shepherds and the post-battle heroes and the fucking guides and their charisma created artificially by computer and the paradisiacal whore to be consumed after work and the premature ejaculations and the framework of the speech and that it secretly frames and the snitching diviners and the brain-dead henchmen in the dark corners of the projects and the corrupt rectors who brandish the Book and the impotent ministers who ramble on and worship put up to auction and the easy prey when the flag flies in the wind and the metamorphoses of the face and the mouse that sodomizes the cat and the lion that loses his mane and the anathema and the list that circulates and the new members of the Moorish baths and the closed door work sessions and the friday games and transparency at the polls and fake diplomas and under-the-counter bribes and the congressmen pimps and the single one at the top who mistrusts even when applauded his followers and the popular base

in agreement and the leader's haughtiness and the revolutionary jolts and the late reforms and the empty basket and the traitors and the turncoats and the paternal reprimands and the wolf's tail and the long queues and the prayer beads and heaven that doesn't wait and the B52's and the panoply of missiles and the artisanal bomb in the garden and the bars of the internment camps and intelligence and the hood and the use of forgeries and the hands in the shadows and primarily the military all branches thereof parading by.
... and yet the perimeter isn't vast
it's bathing in a luminosity that widens it
and the sea
green in its bays tears in its middle

Inflation...
health one has to watch one's health
the children are grown already
and others grow up too many
nervous
champing at the bit in the streets where there's no room left
there are those who return from Afghanistan
those who dream of a boat to Australia
and Baghdad under the bombs
the sea veils itself black
Poverty lies in wait on its pear tree
the satellite dishes are hollow
O the beautiful promises of yesteryear
your plans are totally wrong

You mustn't believe...
my tribe which nothing sways doesn't stop
despite the successive droughts and a hurricane of fire
to brag about the deviousness of lovers
to prolixly describe the border Customs it goes through...

The sea it
inhabits a shell   remains a wild
beast in the story

Paris–Constantine–Paris 1992–1993

EMPEDOCLES' SANDAL

Das Land, wo sonst die Purpurtraube gern
Dem bessern Volke wuchs und goldene Frucht
Im dunkeln Hain, und edles Korn, und fragen
Wird einst der Fremde, wenn er auf den Schutt
Von euern Tempeln tritt, ob da die Stadt
Gestanden? ...
—Hölderlin; *Der Tod des Empedokles*

Traces / Renown / Shades / Urns / Life(s) / Epoch / Zenith / Lucid /
Strangely / Suspended

Stop
a pause of short duration   the closed
space   compelled remembrances   tears
they are not necessary
the dictionary tempers the banality of the stereotype
a nostalgia emerges in the description of the place

like a circumscribed exile
like the eye dimming after the junction

handicap of the code
unusual names at night fall
despite the invocation's depth
the usages intermingle on the asphalt
the trace vainly sought   there   effaced
it is visible
          o heart you weaver
the times don't change that fast their duration
nor the embrace that follows where a soul deciphers itself

a proliferation of signs but
                    the loud voice the one
that unties the tongues and curbs the discourse
alas
    so many lethal traps on the way
the angels refuse to accompany us
the lights blink ostentatiously
the harangues lead us far from the encampment

This is the moment

to enter surreptitiously I go in
my purpose my utterance to open the door
to say under the dictation of a continuous effusion
to align a text without history
for a moment to enjoy the stopping
to reveal the splendor and brilliance of the vestiges
without giving in to the letter's subterfuges

Paris november rue Saint-Antoine Constantine
cité du 20 août Paris again
examine each of these addresses

a small light rift whips the clouds

Itinerary
of precise annotations the return therein
envisaged I know
the tracings the dwellings and the hunger
the hesitation to take to the road is real

renown by auction
victims interrogate who kills and reason

pomp makes sense only if sustained
a hollow word illusions
charisma is not a copyright trademark
danger metamorphoses the limbs
there is nothing to brag about today

the days have become flat right after the exchange
the rivers advance in error in the moonlight
I hesitated a long time before coming
what is man without the praise that precedes him

you he; me for a long time tightly in your arms
without a word
                    the eyes closed I believed

passion an outburst of eloquence   ah
how to get rid of that one   there   image
to put fire to the house   what an adventure
country or metaphor causes prejudice
the brothels have five stars

the city rejects you as you step off the bus
it fears the look devoured by exile
the limitless pretension of the accomplished witness
he knows how bitter all food is
the quick incendiary glance at the sidewalk cafés

elsewhere

there are bars where the name imposes itself
the throat forges a name
customers attentive to the mordant killer wit
beauties day envies their black stockings

neither the bus nor the town hall square have doubts
the lover's glory when the glasses clink
nor the play of mirrors where friendship melts

trajectory   fixed
meeting   inevitable

there is no sales point nor waiting room
where you didn't exercise your gifts in pure loss
fascinated by the tenebrous beauty of forgetting
that grabs the sonorous cohorts in the city
a short-circuit

Lemurs
night escapades
to watch your secretive ways of appearing
from the
bird
in the tumult the thirst
my head will roll at the edge of the river

the bits of green become visibly rarer
the raised walls
                jostle
                        the talk of lovers
the hands unlock at the call of the setting?

black blood revives chthonic speech
it upholds the enterprise of chimerical *periplos*
that quest loudly proclaimed in public
companions perished
                        far from the atavistic
pains of the libations
                that punctuate mourning
from memory to question these dear beings

I accosted my father in the thick of so many dead
unable — did I dare — to deliver my message
I had fortified myself with lion's blood as
the barflies call red wine

I lost my way along the boundaries of the two worlds

in my pocket the right to enter
your coins barely buy one round
the soul of things   can you put a price on it
how much the assessment

moribund rituals
                    reference points
                                    dissolving formulas
windows giving on roofs
open on an ancient canvas that challenges you
access to the sky's colors jealously closed off

to conform to the roads' tracings
giving to the prescribed charities
                                here lies choice
                                        in the programmed debris
                            lush spectacle
                            smiles and congratulations
                                        facade

the complaints of those who are not dead reach you
you know burning hate a secret remedy
...
the long sliding night introduces to the telling
of adventures the magnanimous outlaw hero
the poem carries along since the art of weaving
the assembly settles there as if around a fire
each one dreams of his kin left with no worries
the rhythms are favorable for enjoyable meetings
but sometimes the poet strains to blur
the narration's weft through an excess of figures

the bird that takes its flight at midnight is blind

Interpreter,
the lexicon at work
far in the abyss the wandering gait
no care taken
with the staging neither obscure rhetoric
nor this imperious vanity of surging forth

                                        sun
the instant contains its light — cursive resonance
it dazzles the cantankerous audience you
undecided your gear
slung across your back chains
the house is narrow
you declaim what you know onto a canvas
a sorting out occurs invisible
scattered traces
to describe the table the luminous circle
it is possible to forget oneself in the description of objects while
carefully watching
the precision of the study time
that one's not sparing with embellishments
you enhance the declamation at the risk of perturbing the reception
to catch depends on to the baited trap
the chant doesn't harmonize with the voice
something you no longer doubt

urns preserved the spirits of the ancestors
dogs for the circumstance
the occurrence demands vagueness to the detriment of
urgency the celebration in fireworks
one by one
                all
                        tutelary deities
praise consecrates them at the vault's summit
once the tower has been abolished

obsession
from quarrel to break
the argument contracts then loses itself

in the blackness of the invoked night
system of control
ineffectual despite the forces deployed
the warning shots
the blade
I was walking
up Boulevard Mohamed V. Kalachnikovs firing. The city safe
no longer for night wanderings.
The moon exposes the flaneur to danger.

life hangs on a thread
but the needle and the hand and the freezing lover
at the gate of the labyrinth
fear of the worst hastens the cadence
a breath missing to calm the grief
from the announcements to the road crossings

the blue-gray mysteries of the travelling show

Letters
bricolage of symbols gathered in neighboring
                                                countries
the golden thread imprints on the memory
the one I question answers to no
                                        demand
rigid it invents for itself
a republic in which reading commands
                            summary hierarchy
in the scenery
                        a hidden laser
modern he said
to tread territories made to measure
where the places knot into a tight rope
to live truly
to be god

to claim it loudly

                reckless pride

you the Impeder-of-wind with bronze sandals
you the Obscure who loves to disguise yourself
and I all alone tracking you
lives a concise inventory the detail
adorns the gathering
the fragments are classified
to observe a usage
just as white milk curdles

was it in Heidelberg on a road in Sicily
in Evry or in Mostaganem by the seaside
ill-used infinite
few words carry when the tension increases
alternation of the forms does not resolve much
nor do the *rivets of love* assemble
I remain an orphan

neither wine of Anderin flowing freely nor bravado
at the moment when the clan wobbles
neither catalyzing places a sequence of cast names
nor beauties offering themselves along the way
nor the poetic lineage you claim
nor this hard to decipher manuscript nor
any allegiance excluded
rupture

Always
this array of set-backs
you register
              stifled passion
                    far the epic gesture
the solemn declamations at the tribune

dwellings of Maya Asma Awf or Khawla
recall of pure form
                         era of imprecation
                         the loved one veils herself
usury eye and soul
and the heart's expression
and these memorable debris under the ashes

pangs at rising
                    at dusk a life comes to a close
                                                 a novel
torsion
           the star blinks
                         a town in tatters
                                              screams

you envisage death
                    daily reception
to disappear   swallowed by a mechanism
radically no longer to exist   never
scholastic divagation
the views of the mind deteriorate the momentum of the word
                              the South is wild

there I am confronted by the formulas
ceaselessly stating identity to pass
unnoticed
to sound a fortuitous jubilation
                    at the outcome of   a quest
disposed to welcome a meaning that escapes me
              enigma resolved as soon as stated
              to love, an art wherein to take one's distances
              inside of the unhoped for

they will call your surrender wisdom
quintessence the sterility of the soil
and age adds to the bitterness

Obviously
at its zenith
the law has to concede suicide to the poet
assure the inheritance
                              grandly
there is a truth here difficult to grasp
the tomb is sealed

the beautiful to resay it
the road already traced by a mortal's audacity

rustling of the myth
                              discoveries of listening
                                                            smoke
elasticity of the rays

passion consumes you
                              love roots itself in your eyes
you have handy cliches
                              a large library
advice that succeeds with illustrated examples
and you tremble when the loved one appears
is it a life
            a belated madness
a mystery that isn't one
                              sun or rain
                                          prayer
your impatience unbalances nature
where are you at the hour of regrets

the people get drunk on the drunkenness of the masters
each judges according to his manner
an illusory feast takes over custom
blood transforms itself into a philter
                                          waiting for day
                                          acting
above the head   death   the road is straight
it is not vengeance of a wounded chest

it is not surrender to decline
audacity shatters at the descent of the verse
the clamors feed on themselves
to exalt oneself by your name the torment has ripened

the accent isn't new
                    to recognize
                                        the grace of a flash
                        when the soul shatters
happy
in her kernel a poem constructs

to perish
            the elements fuse
                        by hate or by love
                                    invention
that which retains the guest in the house
that which terrorizes the virgins of Tamim
that which persuades the number

the titration is deceptive

Igneous
the soul in its crystal
the way constellated waves deploy themselves
                                harnessing
ONE engenders destroys yet alternates
he keeps me captive
corruptible

the sweet water in the sea on which the fish feed is not
an irrefutable argument against the establishment of paradise on
earth   other elements of a subtle nature enter into
the composition of the air man breathes   which inserts the
human species into a specific animal category
man is like a weathervane at the heart of the whirlwind
                                    the sky attracts him

Aristotle's disciples debated physics   meteorology
natural science
                    then one did not consider armed struggle in the
cities in order to impose a thesis   a phenomenon that
keeps spreading   as does repression   the system has seized up
to analyze sea water   or to examine the conditions of the ground can
in no way unscramble the mechanism   does that mean that in
this process   it is necessary to sink with the logic of the ancients
the trace of the poem in fragments initiates   formal audacities
   a rhythm pursues you   this is no longer the time to evade
meaning   the words order themselves

the year ends white
        wishes crackle on all sides
from the orient to the occident is it but a reflection
light effluvia when the moon scatters
                                        hail-stones
what remains accessible in the face to face
this country where the violet grape once loved
to grow for a better people, and the golden fruit
in the dark thicket, and noble wheat, and some day
the stranger will ask, treading through the rubble
of your temples, if that's where the city
rose...
this sovereign generosity
this evil which hardens in the apple of the eye
these plaints without notification
a salute to the dead friends

Ochre
maturity, it ends with the day
the questions left hanging

you observe the flight of a flock of starlings
bad news is spreading
from the palms of Bahrain to the villages of Iraq

a tenacious worry
the long crossing from deserts to cities
these buried peoples with strange languages

there are only scattered signs
truth surprises you
at a metro gate

this visible and invisible world is decomposing
science assures the poet of his wording
the risks hidden in the hands' palms
let's leave tears and blood
                              our friends are everywhere
the voyage completes itself
                              by day as by night
all things astounded

Parcelled
out they glitter under the moon
motionless

the white armed virgin flies over the offerings

THAT TATAR THERE 2

Enough! Whatsit, whatsit! Who doesn't have his own troubles?
—Henri Michaux

I.

   That Tatar there waits at the edge of a byway. He's been there for some time now, hunkered down and fretting. He prefers to wait there than at the edge of the main road where the cars pass at top speed. They splatter you without thinking twice.
There are even reckless drivers — the bastards! — who turn around and laugh in your face...
...
A long time ago, a Tatar
would occasion so much fear that it lead to giant pile-ups. The strongest men would let go of the steering wheel or jump on the brake any old way by the mere sight of a shiny black mare or of a gaudily colored banner flying.

Nobody could describe a Tatar with precision.

Those who were running off at the mouth in order to edify their entourage had never approached a single one closely enough to draw a portrait. The Tatars had arrived unexpectedly without anyone knowing where they came from. It is said that they are squat and very dirty; that they devour raw and bloody meat; that they impale their enemies and hang them from the store shutters...
They cities they invade are reduced to ashes because above all they detest the urban way of living...

Of course, all of this were rumors that generated much fear...
But fear has only a limited shelf life!

That day, an motorist stopped close by the rider. It was not that Tatar there (the poor guy doesn't have a mount!). No doubt one of his terrifying genitors. He takes aim and shoots him down. Later he'll say that it wasn't difficult to do. You just had to dare! This incident isn't historical. It has not been consigned to the dilapidated manuscripts in the national library. And yet, the oral traditions never cease to embellish that story.

It is said that ever since people stopped fearing invaders coming from the east, all of whom they call indiscriminately by the name of Tatars. The stories insist on the people's and their leaders' heroic resistance. Piquant details illustrate this offensive reaction that would turn the world upside down and deliver the sedentary populations from carnage...
Yet, despite the iconographic glut, the traits of the Tatar remain completely unknown.
...
That one arouses pity from afar.

II.

A hecatomb literally consists in sacrificing one hundred oxen. Among the Greeks or the Peuls, the oxen is the ideal victim for a choice offering. One hundred is not a number you can count on the fingers of the hand. It is a large number that harbors mysteries. Thus, offering a hecatomb is considered the highest possible celebration because you make blood flow without reckoning the expense...

At the moment of their unsystematic expansion, the Tatars offered hecatombs. When they seized a rebellious city, they cut off the heads of everyone, with no exceptions.

The Tatar didn't know how to count.

On the market square they stacked the heads up high. Poured tar over them. Then they would light the fire.
In those days, they did not distinguish the factory from the mosque when it came to relieving themselves. Stage of prolonged barbarism.

...

In the middle of the steppe, the Tatars never worried about anything. Except for their kin there were no people on the earth and oxen were not familiar animals. They practiced decapitation because of a lack of imagination rather than out of cruelty or to gain the good graces of some tutelary divinity.

The Tatars only passed through with the storm...

Their chronicles are poor. They were falsified when they were retranscribed. One learns little of their myths of origin, their shamanic cults, or the outstanding events they glory in.
Those who became Islamized after the defeat of Khan Hulagu have lost nothing of their bite.

That Tatar there, at the edge of the byway, is not the best example of his nation. He has forgotten everything of (or pretends that he does not remember) the satanic rides of his feared forefathers.
To see him there, crippled with rheumatism, one could wonder what is Tatar about him. He asks himself what he has done to God to have earned such a miserable fate.
...

His gaze lights up by accident.

III.

Ordinarily, that Tatar there nomadizes around the Kremlin area. It's a lively quarter and quite cheap where he loves to hang about. He gets supplies at the Chinese drugstore, clothes at the Bendaoud second hand store; for presents Tati does the trick. There is also a biweekly market.
There are many Tatars in the area.
Who respects them?
He has heard that the Tatars were the scourge of God.
A calamity!
They remain that, even if their leaders no longer terrorize the nations.

What guerrilla leader would reach
Timor-Leng's ankle?!
The latter was prepared to *"change the circular course of the stars"*
with his throne in the middle of *"a scarlet cloth."*
...
Skulls split with an axe, bodies cut into small pieces, eyes put out, breasts
torn off, genitals mutilated, all such imaginable abuses create more anger
than fear.

The elements are not unleashed as once upon a time.
...
That Tatar there comments on the daily news. He soliloquizes while
scratching his head in front of the newspaper headlines.
...
Bits and pieces run around his head.
Suddenly, he's in pain.
It is caused by a spiny
ball that
every Tatar carries deep down in his throat
or chest.

Early on
everyone learns how to tame it according to their abilities.
He knows the symptoms. He knows how to time its occurrences
and make a prognosis. He feels it coming on.
He carefully monitors all its beats.

And yet, it has no name.

In winter he does not like black ice. He drags himself with difficulty over
the sidewalk. Suddenly conscious of his solitude and of the cold. One has
to walk for miles to meet other Tatars. The places where they gather are
always far away. In leprous no man's lands. Thus they can exchange news
safe from inquisitive ears. They keep their secrets despite the windy drafts.

That Tatar there suffered many misfortunes.

He forbade himself formal complaints. He doesn't want anything to do with the police. He knows how the police proceed. He prefers to bide his time.

He tells himself that the city is frivolous.

He clenches his teeth and meditates on how to get out.

IV.

That Tatar there listens. He knows how to listen well. Since his earliest days, all he has done is lend a docile ear. Enough to give you a stiff neck. He was never given the right to speak. Not even to spell his own name. Long ago his ancestors believed they were the only ones in the world who knew how to speak. They always began by cutting out the tongues of their prisoners before they cut them up into little bits. They strung the tongues on horse hair thongs and hung them around the necks of their mares.

...

He can't bear listening to those horrors anymore.

His folk rarely told such stories. They inquired about the exchange value of foreign currencies. They compare the price of Mercedeses. They play lotto. They bet on the number of beers consumed. They try to outdo each other with proverbs and swear words. They quibble about the ninety-nine names of the Lord...

They swoon when you recite love poems to them.

...

He doesn't spend much time with them. A combination of circumstances. It's not as if he didn't belong to the pack. He doesn't try to be different. Maybe a bit withdrawn and cagey. Yet, he questions himself a lot. One question keeps bugging him: What happened to turn the Tatars into such scarecrows?

He hadn't dared ask his father.

Now his father was dead.

His illiterate mother keeps harping on the same sordid and noxious stories about pulverized families. Bottom-feeding sagas. His brothers and sisters have quit the tribe.

...

He would very much like to give vent to his feelings. He doesn't know how to.

He listens. He hears everything.

He picks up when words don't make any noise.

The intensity of what is said doesn't escape him.

He can tell poetry from prose. Its characterizations seem obvious to him.

From time to time he frequents the *Maison de la Culture*. Renowned poets are invited there to read their texts in public.

It's always interesting to see poets on a stage.

An emotion makes the rounds.

While listening carefully to them, things are not always clear.

That Tatar there does not look for an answer. He avoids becoming sick and just wants to have a good time.

...

When the words hit hard, he lets out a sigh.

It's shocking!

He doesn't really control himself as he would like to.

V.

   That Tatar there knows his classics. You can't get a truncated reference past him. His cultural knowledge is solid. It allows him to foil the ruses of life's palimpsest.

Be that as it may, that Tatar there is surprised.

Each time he lands in the home country, he takes it right on the chin. Nothing resembles what he had imagined during his peregrinations.

In the morning he takes a stroll around the Square of the Camels.

It's a souk well-stocked with the latest cosmopolitan fashions: suits from London, Italian shoes, American jeans, blue work clothes from Marseilles, perfumes and cosmetics from Paris.

How to explain the concentration of so many major trademarks on such a small perimeter?

All of it drowned in Taiwanese fakes and detritus.

The main drag behind the theater houses the peddlers of birds, bird cages and bird foods. Be it toothless old man, woman wrapped in her black veil, adolescent with face ravaged by acne, all of them display one or several birds for sale. There are canaries, nightingales, parrots, robins, budgies, swifts… Each one praises, for the connoisseur, the quality of the language of his birds. The conversation of birds is highly regarded. One needs to know how to elbow one's way through the crowds of bystanders.

Further away, on the Square of the Wool, some dudes brandish panoplies of gold jewels set with gems, all the while mocking the theories of scientists recently promoted to be senators.

The city is teeming.

The Tatars are true show-offs but nothing's good enough for them!

So what kind of guys are they, over there, as gloomy as the labyrinths of their lanes and cul-de-sacs?

They pretend to observe the moon. Childish impressions mark them for whatever time's left to them to live…

That Tatar there drowns himself in the crowd. Who recognizes him? He can meander at ease towards the butchers' stalls. A merchant is shot down before his very eyes. All he saw was blood gushing. Suddenly the place is empty. The stalls look dull in the silence.

At nightfall nobody stays outside. The curfew has been lifted but the habit has taken hold.

Before going to sleep, the women coat their necks with flavorless oil; they put on their best finery.

At night, the nightmares sneak in. All the lamps are extinguished because of the superstition that *"the great obscurity annuls the world;"* it unties the tangled skein of fears stockpiled during the day.

Sleep's intoxication is inconceivable any other way.

…

The next day the Square of the Camels fills up again.

The bird business starts up at an early hour.

The Tatars greet each other as is their habit. Each one insists on paying for the coffee or the lemonade.

On the Square of the Wool, the grilled sheep heads exhale enticing odors...
Gossip flourishes.

With Ramadan in the offing, prices will rocket.

VI.

The Tatars squabble all the time. They never run out of pretexts to brawl. Their touchiness is seen as a congenital defect. They glorify in it. Twice a year they reconcile around a laden table. The repast is washed down with honey. After the coffee, they congratulate each other in a sententious manner.

The Tatar language is ancient.
Its lexicon rich and varied.
Its grammar has a logic that leaves little room for exceptions.
Its alphabetic writing remains an unfinished bricolage.
The Tatars venerate it.

It is the official language for discourses. Some fanatics want to impose it under all circumstances. It turns into a source of tensions.

Lovers, as a precaution, use a foreign language when they address those they desire.

The Tatar language introduces interlocutors from the word go into the matrix. How to take one's distances?

There are some who claim that it is grating!

That Tatar there doesn't make daily use of it. He lives elsewhere, with other constraints. He is respected because he keeps his word.

It happens that for several weeks in a row he bumps into a word. He no longer finds the formulas of tenderness murmured over the cradle. He asked himself how one congratulates the newly wed and how one expresses condolences to a dear friend or a distant acquaintance.

He searches every nook and cranny of his memory.

And realizes how crushing exile is.

VII.

That Tatar there naps at the edge of his byway. He invents stories to pass the time. He recites Portuguese poems at the top of his voice. He does not know Portugal but he spent a long time around the building sites around Paris. He does not owe his perfect knowledge of Portuguese poetry to the company of unskilled Portuguese road workers — some of whom recited the Lusiads in their entirety.

These immigrants were before all consumed by a sort of blues they called "Saudade." The songs that expressed its sadness were a kind of warning against the temptation of traveling. The taint of exile was indelible. It's not an easy way to get cultured.

That Tatar there faithfully listens to France-Culture.

In fact, it is Mhand, the manager of the Bar of the Town Hall of Kremlin

who is a radio fanatic. He passed the virus on to him.

There's this comedian who is particularly good at reading Portuguese poetry. He's got him figured. A timbre that tightens his guts. He never misses him.

He often plans to wait for him at the exit of the studios so as to thank him for his readings. He would certainly accept to have a few drinks and talk with him.

That Tatar there is alone.

With age travel makes for difficulties. His eyes close to what surrounds him. The spectacle of the world disgusts him. He searches for a long time for the words to say what's the matter with him, without coming to a conclusive result. He tells himself that he is reaching his visceral limits.

He finds that, deep down, the Tatar poets take unnecessary risks.

VIII.

That Tatar there drinks a lot. He is not a drunkard. Alcohol calms him. He needs to drink so as not to get depressed. He examines the ditch at the edge of the byway. For how long has he been here?
He doesn't feel well at all. Nauseous. Is he going to vomit? At times the alcohol makes him reel.
He doesn't dramatize his situation; it's in no way exceptional.
His family, he doesn't talk about. The Tatars rarely confide.
…
They accuse them of being horse thieves. They keep an eye on them.
They pretend that you have to expect anything from them.
…
That Tatar there doesn't seem like that. He sticks out his tongue. He's a good guy! And yet he's a Tatar!
When the evil winter wind whips his face, he finds the warrior grimace of his ancestors again.

The office for urbanism asked me to interview him in the context of a study on migrants.
That Tatar there mistrusts sociologists. I think he confuses us with social workers.
My interview with him was limited to very brief q & a's.
I was unable to get a usable life story out of him.
Before the meeting I had informed myself concerning the Tatars in order to connect better.
He did not like my empathy.
He pretends that Tatars are not people who travel.
They move out of necessity.
A sociological inquiry would only blur their tracks…

I nearly intercepted the gaze of his revulsed eyes.

IX.

That Tatar there intrigues me. I will not spend my time watching him. That's not all I've got to do. There's work waiting for me.

He,
his whole existence is spent in sloth.
He gets drunk on draft beer. He cheats when playing poker. From time to time he dabbles in antiques at the gates of Paris. He stops off in every bar.

A Tatar is good for nothing.

Like all Tatars.
He upsets me with his nonchalance. My attempts at taming him have come to nothing.
At bottom, it is he who avoids any contact.
...
In order to silence my bad conscience, I gather information about the Tatars. My research is laborious, despite my enthusiasm for the work. The documentation is meager. I find breathtaking sallies in a few marginal poets. They make a show of black humor at unexpected moments and reject the image with the symbol.
But most of the time Tatar poetry is too lyrical for my taste. It uses antiquated ornaments. The metaphors haven't changed since the first odes carefully preserved in the anthologies.
...
What is the role of poetry in a Tatar's everyday life?

I've learned from the merchants of Kremlin that that Tatar there dabbles in poetry. That's why he's considered harmless in the quarter. He adds a twist of exoticism to the Bicêtre bar.

For me, he doesn't want to recite anything.

X.

That Tatar there trusts in the cards and in his premonitions. He has ominous dreams but before all he has endurance. He does not despair of finding a solution. He rids himself of all the imponderables that cross his path. He advances despite all.
Rumors at times throw him off.

He regains his countenance by thinking about the episodes of an ancient drama.

Long ago, the Tatars nearly disappeared all at once.

...

He knows that the steppe no longer nourishes the Tatars; that its limited space no longer permits the great treks; that there's no royal eagle left to trace a route in the sky; that the rivers and lakes are polluted; that even the wormwood and the wild mint have dried up...

That Tatar there perseveres in his wait...

All the Tatars are not dying, far from it. Their movements are controlled regularly. It's not an easy life. It can be summed up in a few words. The Tatars somehow manage to eat enough to still their hunger and to improve their everyday fare.

...

He himself is crazy about a bowl of chickpeas with olive oil. On days of melancholy he orders two and lets himself be carried away by a canary's trills.

Constantine–Paris, 1997–1998

ORDEAL 2

On the walls of your sitting rooms hang my sabre's scabbard
and the eyes of my beautiful horse
and turn my shirt into the subject of your conversations.
—Saadi Youssef

Om Habiba was the first who went outside. Without a veil.
She ran toward the victim.
She did not scream in front of the bloody corpse.

He said: this fickle old man
we killed him after a forty-day siege
nobody wanted murder but what else can you do
when your guide strays into the night of lies
and equivocations
never
will our soul know the sweetness of morning
nor the caress of a delicate memory

She knelt down to cover the lacerated
body with the shirt and she wept
softly. As if in prayer.

We watched her
in silence

He said: we tried by all possible means
to bring him back to a more just way
but he remained evasive
kept squirming

Nobody had paid attention to the bloodstained shirt. He was wearing it
when the servants in all haste carried the body into the house. No one
knows who took it off when the dead man was washed. Those who as-
sisted with the funeral preparations do not remember this detail at all.

He said: we had waited so long
and then it happened without us being aware of it
under our very eyes
maybe I myself dealt
the fatal blow

The town quickly forgot the details of this affair. With the new Commander in place, the different parties moved quickly to get back to their rank and file so as calm the overheated spirits. A general amnesty has been decreed. The corrupt practices were going to stop. Return to the way of the pious predecessors. The caravans traveled about in full security. The Friday prayer was celebrated with redoubled fervor. The conquests were pursued with much excitement. That was enough for us no longer to question the arcana of our faith.

 She said: I no longer know how to distinguish your presence
your smile barely dissolves my fears
my heart has become a path full of thorns
I'm afraid the thread will break because of your clumsiness
or because of mine

A semblance of order reigned but confusion
was settling in behind our backs. Someone brandished
the crumpled shirt full of red stains
before a dumbfounded crowd he
evoked the age and the merits of the dead one
recalled the legitimacy of the linage
demanded the blood price
Catastrophe was inevitable.

She said: am I not the mother of you all
how could I privilege one single clan
my eyes overflowing with affliction gaze at you with the same love
I do not try to induce you in error
I know revolt today to be salutary

He said: it is you indeed whom I have chosen to come and help me
for you I start a second exile
but the needed effort seems too heavy to you
do you know at least what a tie is
the distance the lover covers in the desert
to search out a glance of the one who hides
how I pity your hearts deaf to my solicitude

The day grew dark as if invaded by a cloud of locust or a sand storm
from the confines of the Hedjaz. The temperature became heavier. This
was not a rare phenomenon in such a place. There was no great panic.

I only heard one complaint:

Who will defend Kufa when the people of Kufa
when all are massacred who will defend Basra
when all those of Basra are exterminated
and the warriors of Egypt who are devoured by worries
who will give them peace to open the Occident
and what remains of aides and exiles in Medina
of lords of Yemen or of Bahrain after
the defeat of the Camel that will unite them

He said: I have always killed those I loved
I confess to have found a ferocious pleasure in it
But today my haste makes me angry at myself

I wanted to tell you a story in a way of talking of spending time without
worry without reservation nor innuendo without worrying about the
meaning words take on when you don't take care just to hear say like
rocking or humming or simply slip into air's curvature so as not to have
also to insert myself into the tight woof of a narrative
I do believe I screwed up the war is here indeed and the premises of the
discord are recorded in books that have defied the various censorships
unless the story is a story of repetition namely the one of the eternal return
of unavowable desires

He did not know how exactly to say what was on his mind fear of picking the wrong words as if speech remained stuck to the vocabulary in fact he didn't really know how to catch and keep your attention and drag you into the meanders of a story that had anguished him for a long time keeping him from accomplishing his daily tasks and from sleeping he stuttered I know not what plausible pretext discontent with the direction the conversation was taking

You refused to explain the situation.
You had difficulties talking.
You took shelter at the top of the ivory tower.
You didn't hear the rumors of discord
and saw nothing coming from the East nor from the North

...

She had assembled the women of the household
for a good-bye dinner and lamentations
but when the house was full she closed the door
and run to hide in the junk closet
she did not want to weep or eat the meat
all night long she kept her eyes open

My beloved father	*may God bless him*
he protected me	*my brother is abandoning me*
he is a renegade	*I have no son*
to hoist me up high	*the tail of the coat*
no longer shelters me	*I am an orphan*

Men heard the complaint. They did not understand.
They felt distress slowly paralyzing their limbs.
They did not know how to react.
All preferred to remain silent.

He said: I'm right this war is forced on me
I am the Lieutenant you have to obey me
there has never been a stained shirt
the perfidious one brandishing it before your eyes is fooling you

come join me put an end to that rumor
I grant you my clemency
I am the lover the murderer and the ransom

He giggled and then burst out laughing.
He had remembered an old saying.
He told himself that the world was not within bowshot.
What the eye sees the heart declines without reason.
Sometimes an inclination is enough and the gaze carries.
It's not as bad as all that.

It was said that the horses refused to advance in the battle that the sabres
froze in their scabbards that the black and dry ink of the sheets started to
flow ochre that the bravest men were terror-stricken.

Far from the sanctuary he said my soul disintegrates
I left it back when upon your injunction
now I command the troop to follow me
me the one gone astray in the memory of a love
the one who blames me and incites discord
has not known exile but affectations
in foreign parts career promotions
permit one to strut on the grand avenues
of the world's capitals to run his errands at night
and go home wherever that may be
I ruminate and ruminate while looking for help
from you whose heart opened to me without
making me cross the suspended bridge with you
all that happens is to be blessed
I submit
yet I had wanted another destiny

She said: you spent your days moaning
jumping to the ceiling
you're not the only being fate is afflicting

nor the only one stuttering in the darkness
all these people who rant their mouths full of ashes
are unbearable for me

This man came from Basra. An Arab from the Hadramaut who had set-
tled there. He told us his story to warn us of the dangers that await the
immigrant.
He has a daughter by a Persian wife. She had been raised in the bosom of
her mother while he was battling at the borders.
The campaign over, he decided to go visit his kin and to bring his daughter
along, to give her a sniff of home.
During the trip she asked him ceaselessly if he was thirsty and he an-
swered no. When they got to Medina, the girl fainted from thirst. She was
completely dehydrated. She was given water to drink and could breathe
again. Perplexed, he questioned her. Why hadn't she asked him for water
during their trip? "But, father, I did so all along," she said.
Our language is in the process of losing itself, the man told us. Its gram-
mar is no longer familiar to our children. Other sonorities clutter their
ears. Soon they'll no longer know how to articulate.

The story made us think.

He said: one must not be afraid of distance
or of getting mixed up (??)
we will make an inventory and retranscribe everything
so as not to forget anything
the poems that circulate from trace to trace effaced
the sayings of yesteryear sharper than a blade
the sciences and the logic of the Greeks and the ancient ones
we will invent methods to teach how
to speak to those who submitted themselves
we will open the house to whoever wants to enter
and share with us

She said: the sea is a drop of water
in my desolate heart
every day I bury
the sun and the moon without shedding a tear

CAESURA

Do you, after imagining it, recognize the dwelling?…
—Antara

I.

If he comes to interrogate a half-burned trace, he does so impelled by an atavism or rather a jealously guarded technique. He has woven the poem in secrecy. Months of retreat in the desert, at the mercy of the winds, so as to conform to the tradition. Chaffing and the whip. The echo's harshness initiates into tonal ruptures. Remoteness dilutes the blood. That's when the rhythm's fragility is discovered together with a sudden fear of obscurity. He'll say nothing about the shiver in the hearing or the strangeness of the visions. Sound images jostle…
He stands upright to evoke the dwelling.
The circumstance is banal in contrast to the words that describe it.
A complete rhetorical staging in order to evacuate the mutism of the ashes.

I.a.

    The peak wherein exchange and change culminate without the rhythm being broken nor the word polluted.
The time of a breath...
The evidence of the trait surprises you as it would at the river's ascent. A light appears in the suspense. Blinding, but tenuous. The images reveal themselves, all equal, measured by the yardstick of a trace on the way to extinction.
Here and there blackened stones.
Deserted debris.
Another detour to interrogate the time tested remains is out of the question. That ash still persists in the rock leaves the visitor perplexed. Words erupt, lust-laden, making the pommel list. "You slaughter my camel and my honor, she says. I will not give myself..."
You get carried away on the slipstream without measuring the weight of an exile.
An oscillation of short duration.
The report is a flaw of eloquence there where forgetting bounds the name.

II.

    Liberalities. You give and you receive. You raise the stakes. Without stopping.
Upright.
Turbulence of the ritual. To offload gaily. Ostentatiously.
To maintain a lapsed fire, at arms' length, through the night.
The days diminish as the song begins to cover the cavities of the house.
The one you call to is not empty. You sighed. A name in the wind's hum.
Then languid in front of the door.
For a long time.
There is nobody to lend an ear to a conventional amorous discourse. The turns of phrase are subtle. The form doesn't just aim at the feats of equilibrists. Sometimes the echo takes you by the throat.
...
You have even carved her initials into the wood to while away the long wait.

II.b.

Line barely traced... Distance in the blue of the day.

It is not in vain that you interrogate the dwelling. It opens up to the immobile god, with troubling familiarity. As if to point out to you what should be grasped and kept outside of all nostalgia.

What you decipher in the ruins, you do not ignore it — given how fiercely you grasp the travel coat while waiting for news. You abandon fear together with the provisions for the journey. You know that Ma'bad's daughter is ready to sing your praises.

There are three things that preserve life — caravaneer's wisdom. Infinite enjoyment. These sons of the dust knew how to honor a guest and how to distinguish the complaint of a she camel. They paraded, idle and prodigal /spoiled/, before all at the moment of death.

III.

Vestiges — these intaglios crumbled to dust...

For a long time now
our bodies lie in wait of a rest. A wink, then glide silently into the middle
of the encampment. Take cover.

Celebrations...

You imagine a reunion at the foot of a rainbow. How to pick up an
amorous dialogue exactly at the caesura? To reveal the core of one's soul.
To conceal the questions so as not to reopen wounds. Open arms. There
will be enough to eat and drink for all the guests, music and fires on the
rooftops to announce the feast.
Your desire bows the gaze. Like a hesitation...

Lively images to keep company.

Bazaar gear.

III.c.

　　To live is the time of death... There, a new life. Spacing of the staging points.

The erosion of the rock saddens the eye. As on the day of the migration, you no longer find words to describe the rustle that turns your stomach. An inscription similar to this tattoo on the back of the hand resurfaces.

Empty, the sky like the abode and this tree that bends the one who is lost toward the dust. The bird wheels above the skull with the patience of a tortoise. Ostriches and gazelles have fled the region. Everything's in a state of neglect. Broken ties.

Years have passed and wandering has veiled the memories. How many causes fought for so as to test our limits!... So many strangers — counterpart of light — have come to the house...

Exile has left only a vague memory of moving images.

IV.

Is there anybody there? The question does not seem absurd despite the desolation of the place. Come to think, there must remain some soul living on borrowed time. It haunts the vicinity. He has learned to declaim loudly to mask its demands. He has even come to the point where he doesn't expect anything anymore, letting the words speak at their pleasure. Besides, it isn't the words that speak but the manner or the accompanying gaze. The stock diminishes considerably with time. He doesn't dare draw more from the lexicon. What he knows how to say, he no longer knows how to say. He can barely articulate. This love, for example, that is there. Tattoo on the back of a hand. It is there indeed. In the shimmering. And himself at the edge of tears and laughter. He can barely distinguish the traces of the camp in the middle of the ruins.

...

He remembers without any hesitation all the verses of the ancient poets.

IV.d.

Illusory pitfall. From praise, assured subsidies. Remembrance rekindles a desire for intact cups/ slashes/cuts, of saber and lance.
The ties have been cut long ago...
This flourishing language — a delicate weaving irradiates it toward the absent divinity; it chokes at the evocation of a house in ruins. Deserted places, with brackish water, given over to banditry.

You have folded/given in with this fear of returning and of highway robbers — a fear metamorphosed into a clever trick/a wisecrack.

...
All's changed! The wines from La Trappe rot in the censor's grim eye. Good-bye, daily acts of bravado to measure value. So many beautiful loved women of whom there remains but the name like an entreaty to emigrate: Nawâr, Hurayra, Mayya, Abla or Umm Amr...

Dispossessed in the face of death, you call on the braves of your lineage for help.
Reiterating the greeting doesn't commit one to anything.
From the long errancy of our fathers, we have drawn no warning.

V.

There's nothing. Renew the experience? The pain loses all materiality. At the moment of breaking camp, the heart grows heavy. The eye contracts. An empty horizon.

That's no problem! The pleasures of the body are not futile. They illuminate the soul like the lamp of the hermit...
On the Euphrates, the winds are raging to remind you of the terror of a sacred night and the glare of your escapades.

The evocation suggests a few veiled images storming an uncertain memory. Patiently you put the words in charge of subverting the weft of the poem to transmit a breath. No matter that the wild beasts do not leave their lairs to keep you company.

V.e.

An itinerary skewed by a morbid fever. Sham and pretense from fear of examining a banal frame. Complacency dispenses you from questioning, not the burned trace — it stopped responding a long time ago — but the red-eyed one under the palanquin.

"Go away! I'm breast-feeding my baby. You will not suck my teat tonight... and my kin are ruthless warriors!"

When the storm breaks, you have already found refuge under a satiny comforter. There's a long story you whisper to the loved one to seduce her. A story repeated in the circle of the companions to celebrate the exploit and test the words in real talk.

...
Nothing can touch you now that the days hold you up high.

VI.

   She has never left that trace that sometimes can be read in the rock. Everyone localizes there where a nostalgia presses him. To describe her you invoke the trees and the fauna all around. All the villages of Arabia with their early flowers and their gusts of wind get listed.

An ideal geography in which all stations are equivalent. The women of the tribe are beautiful and inaccessible. Violent desire mocks your ardor. With nothing holding it back it drifts into the joust. There's also the red wine and the angry outbursts.

"And love? How does that happen, in the desert? Because people love, before all else!"

The poet trusts in his technique and in the scope of the vocabulary. He has a whole year to accomplish his task.

VI.f.

Indeed, at the end of his assiduous retreat to learn from the mouth of the stars and the wind, the one who alone has recognized his gift to say, comes to submit his offering to acknowledged judges.

The mutism of the trace remains a required beginning. Everyone does what he can to keep the audience breathless.

What is said belongs to convention: the painting of the loved one as well as the praise of the clan or the salacious confidences.

"What's the point? she says. All I hear is disarray and helplessness. An agony. Exile is sterile. Where is life?"

It is here.
When the poem is said and the sentence falls.

Paris, 2001–2002
21 March 2002

RETIREMENT

*And he misses it so much: and to say
everything he loses in the meantime.
And that he will continue to lose.*
—Mohammed Dib, *L.A. Trip*

*Already the country comes through. I
don't stop. I see the road we didn't take
through our face.*
—André du Bouchet, *Dans la chaleur vacante*

Hotel…
Massilia   Prince Edouard   Avenir
                      What remains thereof after the Deluge.
     Places of passage.
Traces

     Moldings
               and gildings remain mute.
Cluttered hallways.
     A sign: NO VACANCY
The address,
one has it from a vague cousin. Pull opens doors.
Today you can't trust just like that.
You settle in temporarily.
A shared
room.
          Residents or tourists, they live there.

They are primarily men.
Each keeps his story to himself.
          Sometimes, he concedes a few scraps.

The territories are delimited
with the precision of a *senatus consulte*. The tribes rub shoulders
but each one distinguishes its routes.

                                                            The time
of the coming and goings left to the imperatives of the reservations.
The seasons too impose their cadences.

The eye amalgamates.
Sees only the outlines of old immigrants to be taken
care of.

— There's distress, but what to do?
Meets with difficulties when questioning them.
          — "Greetings and fraternity!"
A polite way of getting rid of an intruder.

Shards — examining each bit carefully.

The wider picture escapes the gaze.
To envisage it demands ingenuity, an often unsuccessful ruse.

Is it worth the price?
To stir up the city?

At times, the matter disintegrates…

This crowd you thread your way through, limping,   Gog and Magog

Emblematic. A life,
to listen to it…
My father didn't want to.   Never does a stepmother love like
a mother.   We were very poor.   At home,

everyone rented himself out by the hundredweight.   And seasonal
work!
We boiled the roots.   The carob,
what a treat for the child!
                                You needed money for the boat...
Much suffering, much work   the factory   the building sites
    and the cold.
                        The snow eats the toes
I could not bear the north.   Marseilles is better!...
                                    Honestly, I suffered...
That's exile for you!
You die and then you go on living!...   There's the family waiting...
Irritated,   he asks for the key.   Pretexts ablutions.
The manager teases him: "Careful, don't slip!"
The back is already broken. Worn-out all over.

What's the use of talking...
    Throttle one's pain!
...

The room is a boxroom.
                        Freezing in winter, an oven in summer.
                                        Toilets on the landing.
He has learned to fit in...

The staircase.
            Gigantic!
                        He takes a breath.
The body disappears in the ascent.
By degree,
            with held breath,
                        you disappear in the spiral staircase.
Absorbed,
                                    wandering soul...

It's a darkening.   Step by step...   You do not know the
appropriate words to describe this state.   It is accompanied
by a shrinking of time,
while space opens like an abyss.
What holds him back?

There are the prayer times to hang on to so as not to lose
one's footing. Prayer is a gymnastics of the mind and the body.
Prayer keeps evil at bay.
In bygone days
he would drink the bars of *La Joliette* dry.   He'd collapse
Boulevard des Dames.   You came back...
Praise...
The meal is quickly dispatched. It's time!   He passes himself off as
watchman and
zealous censor...
                    The TV evening news call to order.

A tiny salon. Television on at specific hours.   *Canal-Algérie.*
You squeeze up.
Fit out one's corner. There are stools that can be added.
A world of men folded, folded up in a bubble. Fezzes and caps.
replace the turbans. The colors are dull.
There are those who comment and always the one
who demands silence.
Milky coffee or herbal tea   a little extra
Savor the moment
      ah

Grave.   The trajectory throws one off.
to extract a few facts
All facts have the same value, right?
to account for a life.
An existence entrusted to the Grace of God.
There's nothing to wrong with that. You did what you had to
and you go on.

The mistral raises a bit of dust, cigarette butts, paper...
At the crossroads: rue des petites-Maries,
        rue Longue-des-Capucins,   rue de la Fare
              ...
people standing,
       squatting or
              sitting on stone benches.

... Taxis are loading for the airport

Allô, le bled... Allô, la baisse... Bled phone... & co...
       The noose is tightening around Baghdad...
... Grayness...
Chez Jacques, it never stops
       Bundles and packages block the way
       One tea!
             One coffee, easy on the milk! A glass of water!
  Sixteenth day of the war.   Television, inaudible.
The call for jihad restores silence.
The words resound.
When the resistance fighters requisitioned food.
When the army burned the village.   Everything you have seen.
And the roundups in the home   taxes for the revolution
The settling of scores   and it goes on...
              The screen fades.
...

The news hour   the prayer hour

The restaurant a hive.
What's going on?
Saddam came out.   He is taking a walk
through Baghdad.
  Scoffing at the cat!   Smirk...
       Carried by the ovations.
             The emotion asphyxiates.
Tears.   Nobody eats.
The companions entrenched, in expectation...

Victory is possible.
　　　Like in the fairy tale...
...

The images of children blown to smithereens are unbearable.
"God, oh my God... God, oh my God..."
　　　　　　　　　　　Muffled lamentations **oh**

Irremediable.
　　　Bitterness and incomprehension.
　　　　　　　　　Humiliation.
The city taken with no resistance. Scenes of pillaging.
These Bedouins as if catapulted from Pandora's box.
The stick brandished.　　　　　　Jubilation.
The Imam Ali has been abandoned: ... *The ties of a common faith even-*
tually come undone, all things blur, and failing wisdom makes room for
evil's madness, and in the dissemination one sees wandering hordes pro-
liferate, sowing
everywhere the seeds of wickedness...
　　　　　　　　　His eloquence touches.
The tribe is unequaled in ransacking. It is hard and lackluster.
Cash in and put oneself in the hands
of God while a neighbor still makes a fuss...

The eyes blink over a dirty coffee grown cold
To swallow with difficulty

　　　　　　　　　All around

the conversations proceed at a good clip.
to collect tidbits or rush along,

...Pompous documentaries on the patrimony

　　　　　　　　　Gaping openness

　　　　　　　　　A calamity

Recollection.

                                 The words pour forth...

Everybody loves his country.   But at home things aren't going well.

It's a beautiful country.   There's everything...

                      but things aren't going well.

    Here, it's fine.   It's quiet...

        Haltingly...

Of course one loves one's country! But high up things are bad.

Thank God the children are doing well...

So,

to throw oneself into the tale of the pilgrimage

to escape circumstances.

To prettify the journey.

The one who listens agrees out of politeness

avoid an awkward discussion.

Sitting or standing. always in bunches...   but alone.

They stretch out.

    They drag themselves.

They skim/hug the ground.   Arms dangling.

              Or leaning on crutches.   A cane.

At Porte D'Aix, there are consultations.   One gathers information.

              One gauges the times.

They are neither broken nor crushed.

    A little bent.

Folded, maybe,

to better slip through the bruises of the hour.

...

                To complain like Job

To be there.
    The nail of a Cloud of smoke…
          This traipsing along.   To live
is not easy… Make do…   and if it had to be done again?
Let's go have a coffee. Stop all this!

Patiently clearing the way for oneself.

From Belsunce to the Canebière.
A decor
         propitious
               to deal discreetly with one's business.

On a terrace.
A young man fills in the forms

                        b, a,   ba

from: *The Cinephile Ancestor*

(...)

Later my grandfather entrusts me with the aya of the Throne

   — comprehensive insurance —

                 gleaner
                              under the full moon
      inapproachable
to sleep in the fields in a circular layout
exhalation of garlic onion   the disc for dreaming
back then I thought

                my burden light
                the world

                        at thumb's length

Furious embers feasts starring of the eye
intoxications peregrinations sickly persiennes
dreams tanned with haughtiness I shall be free   free   free
free without fear of sinking into a steel city soaked
with blood

Free

but the city leaves one defenseless

The city's confessions enchant at certain hours
Correspondence

                    Direction of Porte d'Orléans

black
yellow
white
grey loves
disappointing
            flights
                        to bleed while waiting
resemble angel   mortal
imposture
my knee
drags
                lost shooting star
                         evening spasm

and refuses
the attraction of magnetic lightning storms
sobs   escapes
dull running aground
in the flood
                         A BAR TABAC PMU
specters

it's winter languor ever so painful

you say: *I'm cold!*
it froze in my youth

                                        I'm cold!

My grandfather died maybe at ease with his friends weary   all
had left the *Café du peuple*   exactly on time for the meeting
the moment had come   the town market empties itself
of the shared face   exchange   contraction
of the vision life becomes confused   repent at times or
venom   the sun is but   a gemstone smothered by
the crimson insistence of memory early   you repress
the monologue and proud   you manage your day standing up
every single day is too much   to complete a century   find
a reason in destitution beginning all over again
what did you think about   maybe freely for one moment
the interlacing of passions dispersion of the soul   exile
remains bearable at the hour when errancy is tamed   you have
experimented with dawn   so much   under the rays of the
tale   but do you know the tears that come to look at you
filled with wonder   by the slight transformation of the taste of
the yogurt the first time you put sugar on it   it's was
breaking the fast   and how many others already to wish
to die surrounded by one's own   ready   I was on guard duty
far away in the east a premonitory insomnia   wallowing in
smugness and   gullible of   fake
responsibilities
too late and fictive
oh
evanescence the legs cold
but
telegrams never get there on time!
…(sobs)

My grandfather lived eighty-three years

Never turn around!
The warning was noted
it must be somewhere among my things
I did not have the leisure to study it
times passes

...dead   praise for you clears
a space
                    separated from living contractions
dead ends
              all of which are not signaled

... I will reconstruct myself without a witness

                   masonry wall
you proclaim serious
                   an edifice
                                   imposing sovereign
struck down
by the sacrificed hair
jet in the snare
night like luke-warm moss
gently wraps around your shy desire
disables all fear

fecund

                   the sugar operates a metamorphosis

(...)
I do not have the prophet's age nor his wives maternal
seraglio exemplary sacred   separated
                                              railway station companion
                                              with dusty intrigue
shepherd to
spy on the jerboa tracking the sloughings
of vipers givers of seed
artemesia a remedy to be picked cautiously
do not jump over the sloping graves
the rebellious stone in the pocket
cavort with the billy goats
careful handling of tricks
ravines
of the Mina in the Chélif and false arm
sanguine hiding places never
does herald interrupt our rude games by reprimands
our thefts in the vineyards   ferocious noon
                                                                archangel

my cousins taste the mealy jujube   not me
rebellious at home
disputer
demanding a new heart purveyor of talismans
expert thrower
and formidable

mares jennies transported us birth
with in head the pursued by a wolf
exquisite roulades/rolls of dust and blood
clots of attentive cravings firebrand desirings

the sirocco carries the evil eye of the bastards
the sirocco forces the amulets of the believers

I remain stupid at the threshold of severe ecstasy

                                                  entrails torn...

the stable
a crazed hand at the moist hour of the siesta

The saint

      the beggars

              — People of the Angle/Corner

    begging bowls
call for country bread in sacrificial splatter
sanious rags of divine wisdom voracious
lame

      ungrateful sorcerers

                — *fous d'amour* —

inaccessible
and violent
who set up in sermons and announcements in gum
arabic mauve spite turbulent shafts
aluminum spoons premise of trances
outside the tambourines and the fast trot
the rallying cries of the clan

then
   the female ovations essential scansions
expensive thurifer powder
there's grain sheep and fear

rain shall fall or the bluff of man shall flow

they take us away fast
— to shelter —

piercing the
threnody
of the one
drunk of
dust
sweating
he shines

Vicious
          frights someday I will tear up your

                                        dreams

sharing your lice bedbugs cockroaches sewer rats
to gnaw at my breath exhausted with tenderness

                                   — leeches

you lend yourself to clever manipulations

it is only
a bad dream

you have to follow the directions
to the letter bring it back up
original exorcism soluble graph I finally exist
in a bowl of water

The mountain can remain immobile when called
like death fixed as scarecrow for the birds
the heart is a breach in the embassies of the night
and ink an acceptable territory after the deluge

White Ash the fissures of summer
valley
the thistle bluish from thirst coated saffron's
haystacks
barbary figs as fences
the seven strides that signal the olive trees
the carob treat alone like a dry tree   confines
in the middle
the insolent racket of the migratory locusts
green flies
the wind that converses in wear and tear
the spring where the fractional discords pour forth
when the flocks get mixed up

school holidays — return to the furnace
                          exclusive ancestral station
                          fond of sporadic visits
                          very jealous of the privilege

A cat and a jar
there is wild
                    honey in abundance
                                        red wheat in the earth
the silos are not impatient bellies
the oven there that smokes

what's to eat

brown skin of fairy-tale layers
I devour my hunger astounded
like a farmyard

I live the countryside the face stung by a bee

(agony

       white to breathe

              an impulse can be made out)

The nocturnal recitations of my grandfather   stories
for a long time preserve my naïveté   for the occasional happinesses
of intrepid princes wrestling with   alabaster virgins
excited my palate in gorgeous country   anesthesia bites
of take-off   the monochord voice makes me fall
asleep

                              he also translated his cinephile virus to me
superb weekly escapades when
here it is now
the bell of the prison
rang
at the end of the visit

clink bars guards misery   all faded away

                              THE SCREEN

monsters pirates trains and Indians   — the news
the sea teaches Ulysses his forgotten   Odyssey
the Philistines mock the contortions of the   blind one
Attila Genghis Khan...   under the sign of the
Pagan
assassins that mix up   the paradises
adventure music songs dances   an extraordinary India

visible fabulous and fragile always incomplete
          for childhood discernible pugnacious
                    wild in the /throbby straight jacket/
                          light and fire

(…)

The
child
is
alone

I say I am going back up to the deck
                    grandfather to air my soul under the mast
gather my defeated tribe in the foam

decomposed organ
deep throat
vertigo

                                        my torn sky
                                        my inhabited house

...
a lasting oppression

and that still lasts
even if we get over

                    proudly
                              the garden fences
suspended to rejoice
waves and cameras prepared for the reception
of the accomplished road and find again
                                        the friend of long
ago unchanged

maybe weep for joy in the embrace
what do I know we have lied to ourselves so much

even today
the opacity of passed days has not finished pursuing us

Groping along

I draw up the plans for a ransacking

                              minutely

trace the itinerary of a return gorged on

                         seduction of booty to be
                         assessed
                         in ingenious vigils

Narrow programming I was supposed to fix myself
there grow and disappear

bring myself to
...

I come back
ALL'S WELL

frequent contact with precarious bedazzlements
blades

Obviously

an ardor soaked in artifice

a love for the word   accumulation
                                        of primitive utopias

dreaded nothings
              manuscript paperwork in rubble
                                        — my dear world

sweepings
coralline combinations
brain-teaser of many febrile nights

a surreptitious existence

                                suspicious
                                bearer of thorns

where
the cinephile ancestor and
the generations proclaimed pure
and the watered eden after the battle

here

rift in the being the friend
effaces himself exalted like a
sun

now I have lived

bulldozers and cement mixers camp on my blackened

                              jubilations — building site
                              the present dirtied in the

hoarfrost

(winter's bad weather suspends the work
rounded soul
you watch the workers wait for the resumption
unable to change anything

                        — white)

Surface
underground   welding
vesperal

refuge   or menace

girded

once upon a time solemn inauguration

      by instinct the animal rears in the staircase

                center

the city irreversible erasure   ether

that's how it is!

Aix–Paris–Constantine–Mosta–Paris 1983–1986
Picked up again, Heidelberg–Paris 1989–1993
Revised, Paris 2003–2004 (Palermo 9–10 Dec. 2005)
Barbâtre, Monday, 19 Dec.,
Le Kremlin-Bicêtre, Wednesday, 28 Dec. 2005
Finally, Le Kremlin, Saturday, 25 March 2006 at noon

PROSE

from: *Sultan Galiev (or: Stock Shortages; Notebooks, 1972–1977)*

On rue des Carmes what can I say things fell apart. The glass was wilting from too much worry on the slippery road, irremediably emptied of covetousness. With one forced blink of the eye, the basilisk undertook the blossoming history of the eden where we were taking our rage, abandoned like an enchantment, for a walk.

A vegetable garden, locked, abandoned.

It was a day like any other. It was war. It lasted lasted by letting the gaze grow harder.

At wake-up, there was a grain of sand dragging its migraine following the winds' whims.

Winds: our country has a wide variety of them, but their analysis interests little. Itinerant meddahs sometimes use them as main themes of badly adapted tales.

(That's how come a cyclone circled for hours for no reason — rough outline; maybe he didn't know the laws of movement. The storytellers don't always tell — malice of saying — the whole truth in their badly rhymed prophecies.)

The circle of legends freezes the march for a moment, then the stick tells the master to stand up quickly. When? A thousand roads, the unforeseen moment, disconcerting, carefully prepared.

And the guide-man rests his head from harrying roads (an epic), aged under praise, on a populated square where the poet no longer orders the space.

Turbulent solitude, a consensual nothingness.

So, let me tell you a secret:

That day Sultan Galiev was reading Diderot in Bukhara, during a silent interval, rushing to surprise the darkening brilliances and the mosquitoes. In those days the town wasn't worth a fly speck any more as it insisted on thrusting up its minarets like bad quality sugar candies. Narrow-minded and -streeted, congealed in its myths (Eternity has two hairs in its faded petals), it barely managed to smile.

Pitiful grimace in the acidity of its cavities. Potholes.

The inhabitants no longer remembered the prestigious past of their city and said the rosaries of their amnesiac lassitudes in step with the ritual words. The mullahs were hagiographically illiterate. The used book sellers couldn't read the old language. Entitled quibblers.

Everybody was saying: as long as the old walls hold up and the rain doesn't seep into our business, it'

s okay.

The town held up.

In silence. The sky was closing in.

There was a morose butt smothering its ashes in the savage abyss. An evasive fountain pen leaking writing tainted by clean humor, with salacious tint.

An incisive *laisser-aller.*

Sultan Galiev was sensitive to a precise style

preciously at a ten year distance.

Reread.

A nonchalant availability.

The moist atmosphere was humming with lazy flies, annoying and green. Nasal sizzling of suras. Crudeness of wire meshed windows, flaking floors, invasive sheet metal; fermentable sordidness.

Diderot was neither a Tatar nor an officer of the ANP and he was totally bored. Bored to stumble.

Sick century. In the sun

eyes closed, all the lacks your absence.

The blue sky founding in acrid luminescence in the middle of a scattering of trash. Disgusting color medley.

He stood up from the book.

Other books where the words hesitate to burn down the town center. *Mà yabqa illa wajhi rabbika du l'jalàli wa l'ikràm,* which made no sense when the verb folded itself back into its root.

Dead leaves to mark the season.

On the balcony.

The Bellevue-West quarter where the foreigners, scared luxury merchandise, resided. The sheep, fleece stained, came to graze the wasteland. The countryside in the nay of the shepherd (impotent old woman swaddled in her drab scarves), from tense high plains.

It was enough to open the windows, to abstract oneself from the gray decor.

But Diderot?

Vertical in the air's timidity, the last gauloises circled the vanity of gagged revolts. This had happened unbeknownst to the magisterial predictions (not without some snags). A hundred flowers curbed their perfumes under the iron rule of the capital order. The braggarts's loutish moment. Ceremonious sepultures, a dictatorial contagion.

The history of Sultan Galiev begins with 17 October, "a vague ministerial crisis."

To linger over all the carefully erased ineptitudes is useless: the world was tasting a passion drama that still dazzles us. A complete shake up.

The old Tatar bolsheviks — there were few of them — had died for the most part before this date. This is a crucial point.

The new generation of communists has been formed in the school of nationalism and of Jadid Islam. Strange path.

(Determined undetermined gazing in admiration at himself in the crazy mirror to the crowd shouting death to foreign ideologies. How many ordeals traversed at dusk)

Mulla Nur Vahitov and his comrades have inherited its harshness in demeanor and, despite their official declarations concerning happiness, they did not believe in optimism (struck dumb by insolence like an alley of cypresses), source of all values. A contemporary fiction.

(Where to turn to hit the head against the rocky laughter in the kāhin's stutter. My beloved, perfumed with crimson moons, how difficult it is to make a clear-cut choice)

Vahitov breaks with the Party as early as 1918 because disappointed in his nationalist hopes for a great Tatar Soviet nation, federated with the Union, but autonomous.

Galiev is arrested in 1923 accused of anti-party nationalist plots.

Vahitov and Galiev's companions are excluded one after the other. Liquidated in an ineluctable process. It doesn't happen by chance.

A letter, addressed to Galiev and taken from the Khodjaev case file, sets the tone for this story, an epic drama in which the roles were distributed according to objective necessities that escape us and will keep us at bay forever, according to the truth of the saying that goes:

When the earthlight drowns the gaze,

every procedure of redress gets lost in its own footsteps.

We were skeptical petits-bourgeois, sincere in their adhesion to communism. But we saw October before all as the rebirth of our Nation, a stimulating sap. Misunderstandings of the Encounter!

The past, our language, said to be the most beautiful, wasn't all of it good to put us to sleep, or perhaps…

Islam has fashioned us in the melancholy mold of perverted dying sands. The fantasy of a horse stealer, said the commissar, made obtuse by a conquering Europe. Eyes veiled, heart and ears sealed. How not to mislay the whole history. To burst that old seduction without delay. Oh to perish in duration!

I cannot bring myself to accept defeat. And we have thirty years to hope to sing, today even, for I despair to sing some day. It's a terrible anguish, comrade. Though we certainly are not wrong to doubt. The political line of the Party is not without reproaches when it comes to nationalities. And all the rest.

And then,

it is the Party's

duty to listen to us humbly,

point out the Truth to us, produce it, though not invent it, and not reject us for in that case we are right.

Right and reason, but everything is for the best in our "beautiful socialist garden." We are the rustic elephants in Vichynski's book of fables.

I remember when we were students in Bukhara and when Mulla Nur inspired our revolt against sclerotic Islam, against the letter,

back then, everything seemed possible.

Now revolutionary audacity has gone to earth and lends flourishes to the pompous triumphalist style of corrupt bureaucrats, something difficult to understand for us. And we are cowards for not speaking up, and follow the tired trend, tired. What happened, for us to wind up loving our impotence?

A difficult moment.
Others will know how to read Marx better than we and transform our world. We have to stand up for that, but what about desire?
The way Stalin's going, he'll take power and those who applaud our fall are numerous, as they will applaud our rehabilitation. Better to bury us. The logic in all this?

"That's not how you water the camels, Saad."

[.....]

He met Yessinin in a select bar in Montparnasse. In Moscow the year Eighteen preserved its zany cafés and carousing brasseries and dowdy brothels and famed quarters. Spicy nights, the last ones to be lived as one-upmanship.
Yessinin was not drunk after a couple liters and the interminable flow of a disgustingly saccharine music.
The fashion was for rough red wine and Brazilian tunes.
He invited Galiev — overflowing glasses, accolades — a sign that he liked him.
He woke up alone, in a gilded hotel room, in Saint-Denis.

Meanwhile
Yessinin, drunk, breaks a crystal glass
a wish and spits in the copper spittoon
dawn says:
it will rain today, *bluesy days!*
and it will wet my breasts with tears and Polish vodka
and lick me like a street whore in a black
spring, no clear-cut season to slip one's soul into anymore!

The poet demanded a piece of chalk and his slate
but Dead Credit on the wall

to be resuscitated a fat depressed raven, a watchful phlegmatic
nepman economic nervure sharpened
the light kept its distances from the clients.
Go drink in another bar, comrade, Moscow's big. You're gray and hope-
less, blind on the pump and pomp avenue of the Great Evening.
From where do the vintage bottles come? Certainly not from heaven, but
from a long practice by the ONCV (Office National de Commercialisation
des Produits Vitivinicoles), but, well, you're nothing but an idealistic mou-
jik, candid manure; a hick lush of a versifier!
What have you come to look for in the electric shop signs from so far
away? Why don't you follow the steps of her who is waiting for you, fugi-
tive, in the neon of the encounter?
Here we have clean public gardens.

Yessinin was thirsty:
> LET'S DRINK, buccaneer
> to the health of ENGELS

Bolshevik at the cash counter
a drop of ruby red blood
at dawn absence in the iris
loving to dress in unease
in day's burned rupture.

He wanted to drink as if hanging himself from the eye.
In the grayness, the ploy took all night.
Galiev, who didn't hold his alcohol very well as yet, had been dozing for
a long time. His jaw became elastic, his teeth exploded one after the other,
his mouth twisted, mute.
He was snoring.

The room was clean. White in the light. There was a sink muddy from filth and a large, pitted mirror. He squinted with difficulty at his bloated, troubled face, on which was written:

> MAKE YOURSELF
> COMFORTABLE
> THE KEY IS ON
> THE LOW TABLE...

I'm flying blind, he told himself.

A few days later he received the following letter from Yessinin:

Unstable chariot today Friday, the moon (unfaithful in its fancy gowns of strong currencies skillfully woven) gets worried, uncertain how to think free circulation as an inalienable right, telling herself fearfully: I did not choose this cultural rubric; why do they put me in this mess, a lapel-narrow authenticity, to unseat all initiating curiosity. I was queen in an exhilarating dream, emerging original from a sound sunset, captivating, and now these cantankerous doctors don't let me in peace to calculate my eclipses, establish my secrets in sordid calendars, exchanged for a few copper pieces at the tiny stands of scurvy grocery stores O wished for trouble of jade eyes long ago ardently my pain animates the round hill at five in the afternoon.
La tarde que dice soy rica como una costa brava Bravo de toda la poesia Poesia sin palabra ni siglo
Ein Sturm
evening in water so fast forgotten halo in the spasm of your beauty. Inexorable penniless rotation!
I was singing comrade Galiev, yes, you can verify my sayings, and I had much success in my village rousing Moscow even as lover, but I no longer understand anything now, howling in idleness. Must be that it's totally beyond me completely congealed in my burgeoning future.
She dropped me without a word, she did, she left me, nailed to the insecurity of a pedestrian crossing that I can no longer forget, to tear her from my entrails.
Sparkling howl the other slapped the bitter beast for having cheated him, gall, unkind words, limp within range of the labyrinth, no tricks.

And I erred, his road found once again, for a long time eyes blindfolded
by fickleness; here's the result,
I gasp in admiration, unhinged.

Bid my beloved to come and seek / My gaze turned back / The Meddah
strains himself into the silence / Not one sayable story /
Destiny this Arab braggart what do I have / To tell it
Look at it
A lie O

I owe you a simple explanation

Yessinin didn't explain anything. An ordinary overripe morning. Good
morning.
He hit Galiev up for a hundred dinars to pay for the train.
Open seas that carry the exquisite resonance of your breasts.
— I'm going back to Petrograd. In Algiers you can't drink quietly leaning
on a bar these days. To dream the bar elbow to elbow with floods of joy
and setbacks. They take the only gay lesson of dialectics away from us.
These gents want to drink in Switzerland and force us toward orangeade
or créponé smoothies. Enough to get a rise out of Hegel, no? You couldn't
care less the Tatars are Muslims!
— You're not only leaving to get drunk.
— That's core. There's also my girl, she's sulking, crazy mantis of my
gaffes. It's quite a story.

Listen: A lily year
        head in the water
        to dream of climbing the mountain
        pessimist to
        look for you
        in the valley of my smile
(You the one I desire in the snow of waiting so as not to die)

Is it okay? Poetry is a tangerine with seeds but if it helps to reconcile then it's called Cosmic Unity! Ha, the danger the poet represents is bullshit; he doesn't stage anything, the rats are on the boat he is watching go down.
 I'd put the Battle of production in verse form if there was wine to be harvested! Alas, I've drunk nothing.
— You don't believe what you just said.
— Believe it! Drink and fuck and long live the Revolution, the Soviets, the *Internationale* and sturgeon eggs. Welcome!
Escape, her most serene slyness.
Yessinin disconcerted.
In the literary gazette, Voroski, a feared savvy weasel, had just written concerning him:
"One of our most talented poets is losing himself under our very eyes, corrupted by bohemia."
He is clouding the issue.
Galiev quickly understood the profound despair to nakedly expose his innocent fragility that ate him up.

(Moscow was indeed worth a field of wheat for him, a twig that had never owned anything. The family maybe.
Elsewhere, elsewhere he cut his hands to sing
the proletarian revolution as great escape
magnificently adorned with assorted desires.
Things made heavy oh to reconquer beauty.
Then a dive to rest up from the mud dragged along a trip exhausting with promises).

Galiev connected with him in friendship while his relations with Mayakovsky and Pasternak remained social and superficial.

from: *The Old Man of the Mountain*

The first street off the Ourq Canal led to Alamut, a neighborhood under demolition...
Why did the building catch my attention?
The fixity of a wound.
Only one window was not bricked over, a strange curtain — shiny polychrome scales – unveiling a large room.
The street was a construction site difficult to access and I was surprised that it was inhabited. Every day I came to spy I know not what on, for with a burning pain I was hoping for you fully. But nothing or nobody ever showed up. No doubt my wait encircled with violence immobilized the air in parallels.
Reticence of a tracked atmosphere.
There were only the Maghribian construction workers leaving the site at five in the afternoon, abandoning the street to a sadness that at the beginning left me with a slight nausea — the guest invited into the hotel room of immigrant workers will feel this sense of revulsion and clumsily will try to hide it from his hosts —.
Eventually I came to love this moment without being able to fathom the reasons why. It was like an emptying out of being, the sweetness of which paralyzed me. Night would surprise me, amazed in the immense commotion of scrap metal and humid earth.
For the longest time I did not understand the trajectory. Under some pretext or other I would absent myself and, with feet in the water, I'd travel the space of a hiding place. I always had a book at hand I never read in. Badra saw through the game after three weeks of shared life discovering refuges. She saw me. A dissection. This taste for hideouts would lead Omar to the absolute absence — a sort of literary projection which unsaps the gaze. He had started by imitating poets he was jealous of and had created a character for himself that accompanied him in his hesitations. Anybody can thus let himself be caught in a dream that doesn't particularly concern him.
An indefectible life, that hurts to look at. And you, to do nothing else but see it. Dressage.
You don't know how to be adult, says Badra.
(success in Nishapur)

Months of watching had made me into a voyeur with a paralyzed soul. A frozen puddle. Salty with no reverberation. For fear that this state would worsen, I decided upon an action.

I went and knocked at the door of the building. There was no answer despite the light at the window. It was making fun of me. The railing was swaying. I kicked at the door with both feet. Silence. The soft street. I picked up gravel and threw it at the window pane which shattered. I hadn't measured my throw.

I heard a flood of invectives and Hassan appeared.

Hassan, to whom Alamut owes its fame.

...

We ordered several beers at the Alamut-Bar, held by a Moroccan immigrant who stuffed us with salted peanuts and chickpeas with cumin. Later Abu Ali joined us, timidly.

They played the pinball machine, drank a lot and read their future in lustrous words.

One evening with nothing to do, they poured blood into a dirty goblet Omar had stolen in a cheap eatery on the Place des Martyrs, for an adventure the uncertainty of which they suspected. Hassan had had the idea so as to bind them together forever, for their meeting had been a long premeditated chance occurrence. Omar drank for entertainment and Abu Ali because of his attachment to the two elder ones who worried him.

They went to a whorehouse in the *Ciseleurs* quarter and fucked (in truth an ejaculation like a razor, Aaa) the same women whom they chose with a throw of the dice.

... At dawn they wandered about the suburbs of Nishapur near the Porte Neuve.

The youth café opened its doors on Call; it was furnished with a long rocky bench set against the wall. In his tiny shop, between the mosque and the café, the Tunisian was enthroned in front of his dough in the ochre of the petrol lamp. A light fog chased the nocturnal blue thus re-establishing the appearance of the empty square.

Omar bought fritters and paid for two rounds of tea. They were alone.

...Then they separated.

Hassan took a brown taxi to Qom and Abu Ali the bus to Baghdad.

Omar stayed in Nishapur, the break of day.

The Old Man of the Mountain will be the poem of the solitude of the white light that grabs your heart like an apparently innocuous pinch, a sense of disgust so strong you have to lean against a wall.

To falter is not the worst impression given that you are prepared for it (...) you have even nervously pulled a cigarette from your pocket and you are looking around to find the passerby who will give you a light...; but what to do with the well-being of the body emptying itself...?

Could it be that the quest is ending?

You'll have gained nothing if you expected something and you remain forbidden, disarmed, disguised like an empty page. The intentions are vain, the attitudes futile, and the results derisory.

You keep busy because you think yourself smarter that most, you'll certainly succeed and you'll prove your worth, then you'll unveil all the lies. You will be heard.

But you know it isn't true.

Now you are fragile and fleeing like your building with no possible retreat, condemned to enact your dreams rather than dream them.

Carefully uncovered clues.

Daunting banality of clearings.

(The waylaid victim calls out to me; you are not there.)

For Hassan as-Sabbah, the inspired solitude saves from dying.

The ransom: the mystical Absolute — the Rupture —.

In the Alamut castle in ruins, he will remain the Ultimate watcher for having confounded god in the torn vestment.

Desert, insignificance of the resumed shadow.

Omar Khayyam chooses nothing. He is bored in Baghdad just as much as in Nishapur. A sliding of objects.

It is in Nishapur that he decides, hardheadedly, to bury himself.

There he is respected as a mathematician and astronomer which flatters his vanity for appearances.

He loves and separates and loves to separate to inscribe in the poem that sweetish painfulness he hides and that will open him to Time.

An anguish he will not try to confront will take hold of him and he will give in to a melancholy which later will devastate the empire of the Abbasids.

Decline, the sublime will pay with and for his soul.
Solitude is a way of being put in your place. A habit. Khayyam will live a quiet life in Nishapur. He had desired nothing else than this planing down of the gaze.

Nizam al-Mulk, there's the hero
Healthy / Hard Working / Intelligent / Honest / Rigorous / Humble / Good-looking.
Full of life, vitality, humor, charm.
Sensitive and open to others, he keeps his distances in the highest functions of the State.
Abu Ali carried his title without ostentation.
He marries Badra who will love him
                    whom neither Hassan
                    nor Omar knew how to love.
Nizam al-Mulk is perfect.
Everybody loves him.
                    Hassan has him assassinated.
...

Badra is indescribable as the loved woman.
...

This is a true story.
Why does it encircle me through the centuries to live again in a desolate dream?

(In Tigditt, when we were children — caught in adventures, foreseeing death at the slightest noise —, a film that narrated real events was always considered a good film. A true story was the guarantee of seriousness and good quality. One could discuss it, even draw pertinent conclusions from it. Unquenched thirst of guiding maxims. One knew that the film was likely to break during the projection...
Even today I hear spectators leaving a movie house, make the same remark in a respectful tone.)
...

I am truth, al-Hallaj had said. And the souls shattered in a trembling. The crowd was deafened. It demanded the gift, measured sign of ancient times.
...

(A strange dream stripped of exoticism, free.)

Simplicity is the long labor of denied evidences. Reverence: a reflection annulled in the dewdrop.

The poets of the Jahiliya had four years to weave a poem that would perhaps go unnoticed because only one *qasida* was suspended. Inanity of the golden threads. The house exploded from the noise of the merchandise. The competition. Today the Mu'allaqat are uncountable, dusty banderols with lusterless slogans, badly calligraphed. Words reeking of cold offices. The masters of writing.

Valorization of a style removed from the naïve clamor of space reduced to a parking lot.

Who is being fooled? And why?

The street is an anguish exploded in the sun and everyone accuses the neighbor of a negligence that perturbs everybody.

We had come to damn ourselves for sharing the same rays of a black sun suspended from a leaden sky by a jealous, irascible, cumbersome ancestor.

... Khayyam turned away from the movement of the Empire, attentive only to his personal pain. He knew this was a major renunciation.

(Let the others stand up. The others.)

Hassan wanted to turn everything upside down in light of his astounding vision. An illuminati!

Only Abu Ali knew how to submit to the exigencies of events in order to resist depression.

The times were tough.

Political life, limited to minor palace intrigues, fascinated no one. The eunuchs made and unmade the princes without obstructing the smooth running of business. The parties survived in the margins, discourse only.

...

I faded out during the day in a scarlet rupture from which I had patiently extracted the intaglios. Thus I thought to banalize Destiny. To arrive at a state of useless serene pleasure in order to approach the words without fear or shame. Too many kept ambiguities anchored the tearful gazes inclined to abandonment.

To go far away.

I left Alamut pretexting my disagreement with Hassan whom I loved.
He had a laboratory built in the attics of the castle in order to permit my research, which he was interested in. He wanted to use my discoveries to establish the accurateness of his doctrine. I did not understand his religious interpretations and condemned his projects because they terrorized me.
I was afraid because according to Hassan we had to die consumed.
I gave a thousand pretexts. Sordid explanations to mask the limpidity of the attraction. Maybe I really couldn't bear the noise or the smell of hashish.
I was scared but did not dare admit it.
… Hassan had tried to convince me to stay with him. Our long discussions tore me to shreds as I had no arguments to oppose him.
I wanted to live in the calm of Nishapur.
An ordinary attachment.
…

The nostalgia of burned remains was no longer the order of the day.

The daily shifted the dream.
I had nothing to do. Like a witness absent in his waiting.
We spent much time at the Alamut-bar. The prices were low and the customers entertaining. The owner spoiled us.
… The customers loudly commented on the latest news: an imminent invasion of the Mongols. Conscription was going to be decreed and the borders were to be closed to all circulation. Nobody seemed to believe any of it. It was more like a way of joking. No customer had seen a Mongol or could imagine what they'd look like.
Which didn't keep one from drinking to their health.
The regulars of the Alamut-bar had invented the Game of the Mongol which consisted in a disguise: the one who managed the most terrifying apparition was declared the winner. For several days weird and unsettling scenes happened. The drinking binges that followed were often sinister.
At that time, the devout did not yet show themselves in public to attack the drinkers of alcohol.
At the bar no glass stayed empty for more than a minute.
I have learned to drink.

And yet, I left Alamut...

What convinced me to leave: an event I would need to decipher later:

Hassan knocked on the door
Outside a cold dark night
Omar heard nothing he was vomiting the sour wine into a silver basin he
was swaying in the mirror
Open Open Open
Hassan was screaming himself hoarse in the dark and finally fell asleep
on the doorstep...
At dawn Omar opened the door terribly thirsty,
Seeing Hassan he tore his robe and started to scream
...
Inside, a gaze was tormenting me. To go away.
When we separated, Hassan offered me a coat.
You will get cold in Nishapur, he said.
...

Who?

The open door, swinging, undecided.

Those two timid adolescents he had in insomniac nights imagined to escape the prostration gaining on him. A way of embracing life, they say. Khayyam was taunted by contrary dreams and incapable of moving. He was bent over under an ancient lamentation, torn.

The air was hot. Not a breath.

The apartment was large and bright just as he had desired it in his poor youth.

He was sweating. Standing before the door.

Come in.

There was nobody—pretext for him to speak of the past.

A story with many overused effects.

Only, one has to know how to tell / how to reveal the mountain in the grain of sand, something that presupposes experience. One patient enough to follow the tracks of memory. And doubt sets in. Gnawing supervisor. Painful plenitude of memory. To sharpen the observation of a future dissolved in tears. Death the moment. How many accomplished regrets, an illusory accord. Oh, inconstant volutes.

… a fleeting table with the contained delights of Saracen orgies.

How many missed occasions.

Solitude is not a good thing he proclaimed as the mirror was shaking but how to take the decision to kill in order to live, liberate the fabulous prisoner of the lamp? You remain with a sedentary sentence celebrating an ancestral folly that deplores what never was. Oscillation. A minutely elaborated character. Elementary. One day everything will become clear (I thought) and with a perverse insistence I unknotted several years to die in order to trouble us with such violence.

Undoing oneself was a pleasure I did not yet comprehend completely. Intrigued, I watched us.

What do you want to prove, she said.

The impossibility of my free will, he said.

She slapped him. He hit her with a ferocity that surprised him. They grappled, trying to strangle each other spitting their hate undermined by desire for each other. They rolled on the floor penetrated one by the other. There was a scream.

I loved you.

And you loved me even more.

You climbed up a staircase and I knew it for the banister scraping for not knowing how I was able to climb after you and take off my coat and speak. And speak. Useless flood. For years this banister held up my drunkenness. An accomplice that kept me from collapsing in tears.

One evening the first step of the staircase refused to carry me.

It was only justice.

Sprain.

So, to speak of the past... To whom.

That night Badra carried Khayyam to the fourth floor. He was drunk and sick. She made him throw up in the kitchen sink, washed his face and put him to bed.

Empyreumata of representation.

A tragic unity inhabited the peoples of the Empire despite rebellious particularisms, resisting the dispersal of the soul. A savage submission to the mercy of a jealousy salvationist divinity.

The states exalted fictive borders without accounting for the wanderings of the subjugated hearts. A family of weavers made their fortune by making flags. Sacralization of an insipid world.

A subjugated writing kept up the borders without gaining adhesion. A magnificent appearance.

Like many others, I no longer read the papers nor the books that received the stamp of the censor and didn't feel any lack because of this, only a certain nostalgia for wasted possibilities.

Who were we, immobile dust in time's cauldron? How many circus-alchemists to resolve an enigma without a mystery!

A bird-catcher was named Great Cultural Councilor for having trained parrots to teach the renovated classical language to the young cadres of the Nation.

Hassan said: History teaches the erasure of civilizations there where gangrene catches hold of a body deaf to warnings... The Messenger is late... I will be the Omen. Abu Ali said: it behooves us to raise our lives to solar brightness, an attire carefully prepared given the hidden god's lack of interest.

And who cares about the price

... My science distanced me from the declared objectives of knowledge, coveted vanity of the mirrors' cold shimmer. I grew disinterested in partisan reasons, not out of fear of repercussions (I had no fear of the police), but an agnostic torment had slowly invaded me. Knowledge was melancholic and I was beginning to understand the truth of common sense, something that had made me smile at the time I was at the university.

My love for poetry deepened this attitude by opening my eyes to the visionary, the reality of days without tain.

Khayyam said: happiness is far from being an acceptable idea for us and it is in vain that I question myself.

...

This morning I went to the bazaar to buy a pair of sandals.
Apprehensive faces confronted me who had very little desire for civility.
Closed. People couldn't stand each other during the month of Ramadan
and anything was pretext to a quarrel.
The street was aggressive.
A rusted blade.
Why fast when the intention is not pure
And all those masks!...
Indifferent to religion, I did not fast, but didn't make a show of it as the
Doctors severely punished every transgression of the law. Islam was guid-
ing the State. The word, enslaved.
The great debate: the regulation of the length of the beard and mustache
so as to conform to the teachings of the Sunna.
Bleached bones. Friable.
I was worried about the straight disposition which annihilates the gaze,
a constructed bedazzlement. Life.
Khayyam refused any complacency that would break his being as he had
no other place of revolt; limpid intimacy.
Like the intellectuals of his age, he had accepted everything.
He had shut up.

An obscure life kept him out of the sight of Power. He earned his living
teaching in Nishapur, a provincial town. He turned down job offers in
Baghdad, something he regretted from time to time.
He was gifted and was often consulted on matters concerning astronomy
and geometry. Why did he always separate his teaching from official doc-
trine. By affirming the objective reality of science he scandalized his con-
temporaries. He had a taste for paradox. Before all he wanted to be
unfettered and suffered from not being able to blossom in an empire that
had successfully interiorized censorship. Troubling façade of disavowal.
Of which he himself was a victim.
He permitted various mystical interpretations of his poetry to circulate
and took part in events without contradicting or taking sides. One thing
only obsessed him: that his work not compromise him in the future.

About which the world couldn't have cared less. He himself at times laughed about it.

...

The bazaar was crowded.

Haggard wanderers. Tattered beggars. Pickpockets lying in wait. Old women veiled with rags. A miserable throng. Bruised space. I lowered my eyes so as not to see.

A vulgar blinding.

Spice labyrinth, dripping tripe, rainbowy syrups. Doubtful picturesqueness of penuries. Vulgar jewelry shops. Poverty.

... The shopkeeper moaned behind his counter. I looked at him, not daring to cross the threshold. For a long time.

What is a man's pain worth?

I greeted him.

Without answering my greeting he said: Baghdad just fell.

He realized my complete befuddlement. He explained the conquest of Baghdad by the Mongols, the end of the proclaimed world. They are the spectators of Iblis. Gog and Magog loosed upon our unawareness. Because the family of al-Abbas was not able to follow the path, to lead the community in justice.

They burned the Burda!

Unhappiness has overtaken the Muslims!

I knew those tales that had terrorized my childhood.

Shivering pupils listening to the predictions. Winter nights.

The Mongols do not exist, I said, a phantasmagoria invented by sick traditionalists. Anyway, aren't the walls solid? What is certain is that Baghdad will hold on our ashes. Resistance of materials. Dust vainly clogs the memory... Today it is the weather that doesn't work, hanging from an extinguished candle. The empire trembles when it should rejoice, free, delivering its distress to the day and burst into flames like the sun.

Why?

We are certainly somewhat deaf, ignoring the simplicity of first emotions... And so bound by artifices.

Listen to your soul, there is nothing to be afraid of.

... are we not in Nishapur?...

He was weeping.

The Mongols themselves are greatly afflicted. I have studied their history but I am boring you.

Console yourself, friend, and tell me who is the Poet
Al-A'châ, he said.
Ah, I say Tarafa. You see, we are alive.
He thanked me, I paid a good price for my sandals.
...
I hurried my step to get back to my observatory. What the merchant had told me upset me because I was afraid that I wouldn't be able to finish my work in time. The Mongols would perhaps destroy it, but that didn't worry me. What I couldn't bear was the idea of not finishing. An incomplete life.
Nishapur was not that separate from the world.
Why had I lied to the merchant?

... I had let myself be caught in the wonderful elsewhere that I had to un-ravel patiently.

Avoid the peacock's deceiving tail fan.

Where

For elsewhere too the Mongols terrorized the nations. Their advance has-tened the Day of Reckoning. Azrael was leading their cohorts, riding a black mule whose shadow was the length of ten ploughs. ... They were ferocious and innumerable.

New beliefs were born out of fear.

The Mongols were the turmoil of our errancy, a narrow turmoil.

I knew the vanity of this clamor that came to us held back by the dis-tances. The exaggerations rendered the facts ridiculous.

Free and accurate news would have taught us to overcome such childish fears.

But who cared about being free.

The pillars of the Alamut-bar still got intoxicated drinking to the health of the Mongols in the doused neon fairyland, reassured by their usual jokes.

Bar flakiness, freedom!

In dream to last a few happy stages for the soul was engraved.

How to rebel against the edifice's fatality?

The bar top swimming in wine, hilarity of a sluggish atmosphere.

Elsewhere had no consistence.

...

Alp Arslan restored the State to its ancient munificence and Nizam al-Mulk organized the power structure. Authority was established despite a few minor trouble spots. Brutality of repression. The Caliph had submit-ted by confirming Alp Arslan in the dignity of Shah. The fiction of unity was maintained and the tributes paid.

... The corporations were carefully controlled. The peasant revolt of the month of Ramadan did not cross the borders of the newly conquered Khorasan. The university was going to be founded anew.

The public buildings proudly displayed by the people and for the people. Glorification of the slightest gesture.

They exhumed the martyrs and the heroes that exhorted youth to follow their example. The merits were exhibited in annual fairs.

Praises to the president-prince, he of the nocturnal ride and assigned land, pointed lance and solid shield, he is the pen that instructs. The Best.

Unanimous agreement.

We had to be on guard against freedom which was a need foreign to our culture, an imported model. More subtle analyses presented it as dangerous, given the priorities.

Alamut was not yet talked about. Hassan was managing his father's business in Réï. At least that's what I guessed, though I didn't have any news from him.

I was living alone, with, at times, the memory of Badra whom I had loved. Whom I still loved. But...

... To the students who came to ask him about his research, Khayyam offered coffee and changed the conversation to questions concerning the love poetry of the Beni 'Udhra.

Why wasn't there a new Qaïs ibn al-Mulawwah or a new Djamil? True ornament of the century.

Purity of meaning.

We no longer know how to love, captives of our calculations. Smallness.

But the students had insisted on the scientific aspect of their investigations. He was caught by time and couldn't allow himself to converse.

They had established rigorous statistics.

Khayyam answered that tranquility was an excellent research topic, though difficult to quantify. He had problems with his coriander, mint and basil plants which were drying up abnormally.

The lack of freedom strangles all creation among us, he said.

I am leaving the discoveries to the weak. My heart broke as one breaks camp, a long time ago... desire extinguished.

Badra was beautiful but so long ago that I couldn't describe her. To say what? Vagueness of the line. Aphasia.

Invoking her my body contracts and even today I tremble as from a whip's bite. I shove my fist in my mouth to break the cry and with eyes closed I force myself to penetrate the inside emptiness my ultimate protection. Unforeseen quaking of strong impressions. Stridency of a rupture. /

A needle without a magnet

A moth panicked by a lamp

A spinning top

Name me or lock me up in an asylum.

... Then, calm.

A tenderness invades me and unties my body to taste you in the depth of myself. Flexion of the senses. Appeasement of the blood.

Badra came back to me in a vertigo.

Omar could no longer remember their first meeting. He was certain, however, that it was he who had introduced her to Hassan and Abu Ali. Badra was sad and Omar wanted to teach her to love life. To extirpate the soft sensation of death her presence emanated. They had a relationship Hassan couldn't bear for the first few years. Hassan entertained a ferociously possessive friendship with Badra that gave him the right of life and death over her, so he claimed. Badra was weary of Hassan's scenes but she cherished him despite herself. Abu Ali had not caught her attention and I was surprised that he courted her after our separation.

The motive? Unimportant incidents. I was in love as one is in a tale. Devastating hotheadedness.

My heart, why are you so mad, she said.

I didn't understand. I loved her. You the Only One, in my gaze blindly riveted to your pain. The lover's savage indifference, Oh my love. ... Will you forgive?

I was already tired in my dream. Unforgiving latency. Upon waking up, a table had been set where I had to sit down obediently.

...

After lunch Omar decided to write a letter to Badra:
What then did you know not knowing the love I have for you, eyes closed in the mirror. Each day separates us more, evidently, my loved one; I miss you painfully for no longer putting up with you gorgeous with desire.
... He didn't know what to say.
To tell her that certain nights I rage to bite her though the moon's blemish isn't the cause for it.
To tell her the softness of her skin that troubles my hands.
To tell her that I kill and mutilate her like a child jealous of its toy.
To tell her how I wake her.

Words Khayyam didn't know how to link.

... Then he gave in to the poet he loved:

"Our love was this:
it left, returned, brought back to us
a lowered lid, infinitely distant,
a fixed smile, lost
in the early morning grass;
a strange shell which our soul
tried to decipher at all times.

Our love was this: it progressed slowly
Blindly advancing, touching the things around us,
So as to explain why we refused death
So passionately.

No matter that we hugged other waists,
Threw our arms around other necks,
Desperately
Mixed our breath
With another's breath, no matter that we closed our eyes,
Our love was this...
Nothing but the very deep desire
To halt in our flight."

Nothing to be added to that.

Will she appreciate it? In the past, they drank the same water. Khayyam felt safe behind the at times pedant display of citations. He knew many. Each circumstance was an occasion to recite a poem. Never his own, which he was incapable of committing to memory.

At that time he was very serious.

You want to have it all, the children reason thus

… I would like to die, she said

Certain scenes persisted.

Insistence of moments at their effacement.

Disappear!

You have hurt me so badly, she said, and you are not even conscious of it.

We were alone, desperately — succession of troubles

A medallion

I had forced the circumstances to weep over the separation but the tears that hollow the dream are real.

Khayyam: The past is a cannibal living in a clearing

Hassan: The forest is our savior, lose yourself in it

Abu Ali: One does not go at the world with images.

Only images were given us as consolation.

from: *Ordeal by Bow*

(...)

We'd wall ourselves into these beer halls — the Ya-Sin Brewery, the Peepers, Chez Abu Nuwas, the Four Arts — close by the university, or into the Eighth Wonder, a passable dive where the kemia were varied, not far from the National Library, very late after legal closing hours. Every evening the same evening...

The curtain drawn on an acrid intimacy: a sort of accord of accolades, breathless kisses and repeated slaps on the belly, hahaha, and more cuddling and embracing, and on top of that affable arguments. A vigorous joviality was the sign that we liked each other well and that life was good all said and done... Intemperate boars. We were lazily wasting away among the sour smells of alcohol and urine, the stench of vomit, the room's tobacco saturated atmosphere, the foggy brouhaha... Intoxicated tremolos.

It was enjoyable disgust, ongoing, in spirals...

The head foundered, full, it reeled in technicolor, it emerged with one detail blown up, bizarrely questioning, and it would then disappear, soothed, up the gurgling gut. The eyes would fill with tears, hot tears voluptuously coiling up. It was a liberation into an ephemeral flowering in the suave mist: it made rainbows capping the city like at the lion's wedding.

Fringed silk scarfs.

... The wall paintings — still lives, imaginary flora, hunting tableaus, portraits of enticing women, polished allegories, scenes from a *mauresque* Paris, hodgepotch of fishermen's stuff, tattoos, etcetera — screamed their idiotic naiveness, pretentiously claiming to brazenly manage an artistic ideal gathered from some magazine. Certainly these paintings were inspired, given that the artist was paid with free drinks; still, they remained conceptually mediocre. They did not manage to translate for the spectator that exalting thirst of the privileged moment that saw them being born. Demented daubs.

And yet they forced our gaze into a contemplation as absurd as it was rich in harsh, unpredictable emotions. The dreaming eye always disconcerted, even though dozing. These paintings were signed and dedicated to a favorite mistress: Aïcha, Georgette, to the loving and Unique mother — majestic Piéta — or to time's rigorous treason. Ogre Cronos dreams of crocs. Depths, long and large, ah! Time! Time! Always!

...
A là ayyuha dhà lla'imî...
fa'in kunta là tastî'u daf'a maniyyatí
fada'nî ubâdirhà bimà malakat yadî...

It was the pure product of a shared experience: an impromptu suite of black misery traversed by lighting bolt clearings. One had to go to the old ones, the one growling before a table heaped with corpses, and ask them humbly, so as to realize: typhus and the hail of frogs and the rationing cards and the Americans and bombs of every description and the *indigénat*: thus, untamed, blue jokes come at a price.

The teary colors, ungainly, muddled, of what were paintings covering the walls: crappy yet lachrymal, opening up in a tightly wound labyrinth, a minuscule network of outrageous inspirations, of erubescent wonderments, carnivorous alveoli, a labyrinth like any labyrinth imperiously tempting my curiosity, and on certain evenings totally captivating me... I would let myself get silted up like an old boat or a sperm whale tired of running from that harpoon launcher; I'd negotiate an ecstatic rendition, but he, sentinel at bay, octopus proud of its refinement, would keep me back each time with some mordant remark, not hesitating to crush my toes to keep me from diluting myself in the formless, as square as the public at the foire du Trône in their Sunday-best — the flabbergasted circle of the Place de la Bastille — a bystander's exigency and appreciation.

He was gifted for a preventive critique against preposterous ecstasies. He had the cynical *voyance* of unleashed good taste's intransigence, the manifestation of a polymorphously sacred that kept him quite taut and tight in an ivory-esque solitude he boasted about loudly, but which I suspected to be but a protective facade. He needed that distance so as not to let himself be importuned by the failing movement of nature matriculated in the discretionary administrative services. Keeping at an absolute distance.

Starchy disguise of a patented nuisance! A small patch… me, I quite liked those pompous paintings. They had a great effect on me. As if familiar, they hooked me into a faded memory, an impression that didn't come from any reading. They truly moved me like things already seen with tenderness or, better, as if I had already often lived through these moments of contemplation. It was like the palpitation of the migratory inspiration the eye's pupil found again, intact. There was a touch of nostalgia.

Oh, indescribable limpidity of surreptitious effusion.

I experienced a childlike pleasure seeing those paintings when I raised my eyes from my glass, would salute them cordially with a toast. I confided in them.

They were at their place.

….

And, laughing, I imagined no other pleasure than to drink unhurriedly amidst such hypogeal illustrations of our salient feats.

…

So as not to give in too quickly, (because he, the critic high above the mud, would scold me nastily! Something I didn't much like)
there was first of all my nose,
there was also my ram-like stubbornness,
there was also the fact that I became quite taken with the game and wanted more as do all gamblers when the demon wakes up,
I would begin to finesse (I was capable of that!)
… I would haggle over my misappropriations.
Stirred up by his haughty gibes, I'd take off on a tangent and prevaricate in order to measure the gradations of the meanings. I took my time…
And he would take refuge in emphasis…
— You have to drink without hesitation, goblets and liters, as long as the liver works for the organism won't always assimilate the alcohol, he'd say; a liver is not eternal, nor are drinks! For decency's sake, avoid to drown too early in aesthetic phantasmagorias, it's phony. Humans, oh the poet knew, in his agony, having had a rough time of it, braying to shield himself from the whiffs of camphor: bring drink!

Pour /and pour/ and pour again the circle tightens untightens retightens /already/ disperses /beat of a wing/ grab in mid-flight my fire is thirsty / to death / thirsty my earth shaven   consumes itself dawn   deserts its source ... azure permanent ensmokes me   quick! barman fill the glasses to the brim, pour...   the wine the souls on the bar scatter (nothing lasts and the eye leaves) sip after sip after mouthful I swallow drunk I want to succumb in beauty

There was a short silence, despite all! Then...
— I drink and persist, I say ostentatiously raising the stemmed glass; but that doesn't keep me from looking. I got the means. Nothing doing, compadre, you're on the wrong track; keep your verses. I am lucid. I love! I truly love, and, like you, I have learned that *"this century's poetic sighs are but sophisms"*!
Wind!... What do you want? I love!
He says: drop it! To love is not to be delighted. It only entails low work, acrimonies and animality in heat. To love isn't a big deal, why be a dumb ass? I say: No! No, not at all! You don't get it. You don't understand or else you act stupid. Love for me is fitting and exquisitely licit. I sigh with pleasure and get all trembly without being able to say what's happening to me. I don't want to dry up inside my skin!

... He was looking for a witness to take me to task and the argument would flare up again and keep going; it would amplify, drag on, calm down, start up again, get all twisted... The drinks would be refreshed continuously...
He, spreading himself about: in the palace of Culture and in the Ibn Khaldun amphitheater, conference follows conference, all of them instructive. You learn a lot. Just think, in our golden age, we invented gunpowder! Baghdad was the metropolis of the world and Paris but a village of dumb peasants! The musicians were virtuosos, not the mediocre strummers one sees on t.v. today, they added strings to their lutes, discovered harmonies never heard before, they thumbed their noses at the canon. They were audacious, back then! Caliph Al-Ma'mûn, the light of his time, presided over the scientific conferences with the agreement of the university corps. He would gather the writers and philosophers in his palace and amazing all-

night controversies would ensue. At the table, the repasts were accompanied by a special vintage with a honey'd aroma. The doctors were dissecting live elephants and practiced organ transplants. Hospitals were free. Books were well printed, on beautiful vellum, with superb illuminations and extraordinary luxurious bindings. Arabic was learned all over the world. Arabic was the language!

The witness: ah!

I: hoho!

He: yes, and linguistics was the Arabs' crazy hobbyhorse. If you look closely, you'll see that I'm not the only one saying so, all of Chomsky is prefigured in the writings of the imam al-Jurjānī. The books are there, all that's needed is to read them attentively... But we didn't last long, because of the crusades and America.

I: to the contrary, we lasted and lasted! Go study your dictionary! Your crazy pony looks to me much like a kamanjā! Old friend, you should know that the only powder the Arabs invented was the one you take!

The witness: oh, yes? I'm not following you, I'm totally lost. I know nothing about music or firearms. I always wore the dunce's cap in my Jules-Ferry village school, always had to stand in the corner, and yet Madame Garcia, who was a good teacher, did everything to make me learn and she didn't spare the ruler. Poor Madame Garcia, I barely can read today...

He: ... We also invented the zero and the mathematical infinite. Algebra and the x as function of the unknown. The numbers, which we don't use. And we also invented the astrolabe and the compass. So much so that Charlemagne, him of the flowery beard, organized a council instructed to deliberate on the nature of these inventions because the Franks were afraid that they were the work of the devil. Oh, what didn't we invent! Europe knew neither public illumination nor the precise divisions of the hour...

A neighbor: stop, brother, stop, have pity on us, those were other times! Alas, today we can't even wind up the clock of the main post office! All the watches in the country need to be fixed. Where do you think you are? You don't live here! You're high. The State swaps clock-jacks when it's flea market time, tickers made in Hong Kong and Taiwan; it steals our time through monstrous wastage, and we love every minute of it as it provides an exculpation that fits us like a glove; the State's a monkey on our backs constantly bugging us rather than sending us into space. And you speak of precision!... (the time to down his drink)... Are you not part of the common lot? (...eloquent pause). Cousins, please, for the sake of the drinks we shared, enough already, stop it with the grandeur of the Arabs! Enough about usurped splendors! Stop it with that one-eyed past! It's a calvary for the ears! Does this heritage put food on our tables? What is it, anyway? A fraud, a con! Speaking for myself, my grandfather has left me a family tree that goes back all the way to Ali and Fatima Zohra, on a piece of twice-folded kraft paper, full of grease stains, with nearly illegible writing, but when I go back to the tribe to see my uncle who is a marabout, he too owns a copy of our genealogical tree handwritten by the master of the *za-wiya*, but the hunger is still there! And our rags are shiny with dirt and fleas. Of course, it's not as it was before, but what does that change? The Arabs are a catastrophe! A dirty race! Ha! By God, we are in bar, after all! Watch your manners! (… out of breath. A silence!)…

Please excuse me for interrupting like that, so loudly, but we are among brothers. No formalities. You'll have a drink, my round, yes?

…

The witness: all that's needed to start again like before is willingness. The traces of our illustrious ancestors are still legible. I may be illiterate but I did listen a lot to Si Mokhtar, the scholar who was the favorite student of sheikh al-Oqbi. He always insisted that willingness is the only thing that counts when confronting difficulties. He even said that willingness could make God change His decisions. I don't remember everything… We have to make an effort, get a move on, overcome our lethargy… It's France that has put us in such a state!

A voice from the back of the room: a.b. abc. d. down with the army, the abattoir, the bums clowns dickheads. abc. abd. drinks drinks drinks. Too many dickheads here!

The neighbor: come on, this round's on me. *Patron*, one for the house!

He: come on, drink up! Let's all drink! Let's resuscitate! Allah! Allah! Un-worthy legatees of our prodigious ancestors.

I: what ancestors are you talking of?

The waiter, swiping off the table: hey! Me, I'm of the Aouadhias, and that's no joking matter! Careful what you say, gentlemen! Words aren't just words! Where I come from, we dig up the rifles when the name is questioned! The ancestors are sacred.

The neighbor: Come on, brothers, what did we say earlier? No politics, right?! We make ourselves sick stupidly. Tearing out our hair like monkeys. Biting our nails. Worried about nothing, for nothing. What does the lineage matter? There are spontaneous generations, something genetics can't deny.

All summer long we yawn our heads off. We are slowpokes in the rally race of the nations. We are doped up on eucalyptus syrup and aspirins. Star wars are declared way above our heads, way up in the stratosphere, but we are in the cross-hairs, in missile range, do we realize this? Our representatives certainly don't! Reflection is lackluster. The books, pale copies. You sneeze on the dark mirror. You look for adventure, a way out. You organize a pointless shelter. The lamp illuminates only very weakly. And there we are en masse questioning ourselves in that circle of light! We are less than the ants at the foot of Solomon's throne. Morons! It's the international division! Spoliation and terror! The good old law of the strongest! What does it matter, yes, we are independent, but we are not free, and before all we are totally incapable of ever getting along, locally pursuing old homicidal habits. The Arab Nation! That feat isn't worth a rabbit's fart! We shout abuse at the pack. We damn the circumstances. We renege on our words. We are all prisoners in our countries, squirming with unease. Morons! That a public kiss freaks out! And they blab genealogy! We sneak away at the smallest occasion… (Stops, to catch his breath). Ah, so now I'm losing my temper! And turn into just another barroom haranguer! A Cicero revealed by wine! Shit! Enough already. To your health, gents! To keep turning this stuff over only wastes the pleasure of drunkenness… It is said that God himself weeps because He can't be present at our take-off anymore. Bah! These things have been going on since way back when, we are well placed to know this, but fundamentally they won't last. We are the best! We prevail over everything, everywhere. Cheers, my friends! More, more, fill my cup to the brim! It runneth over! Good! Now smash it!

I, in rapture: we are blessed by the fig tree and the olive tree and the vine. To top it all, we have the oleander to crown our foreheads with. But you wouldn't think so seeing us all here wizened in front of the central heating. Are we to deny the benefits that present themselves?

He, saddened: Nothing of us stands out. We are missing what's called the Look. That's fatal. Given the circumstances let us agree to drink as much as is possible while keeping the class safe from drowning, there's nothing else to do.

The witness: in fact, our Prophet, prayer and peace be on him and his, never forbade us to drink; never! God's commandments are subtle, isn't it so, God! Isn't paradise criss-crossed by rivers of wine! And the blessed will be offered "*a rare wine to drink, sealed with a seal of musk… and mixed with the water of the Tasnîm.*" The verses are clear. But He forbade drunken binges, and he was right. Knowing the Arabs, it's obvious! Guzzlers! No style, no manners, no reserve. Beyond that, it was an anti-imperialist boycott.

The neighbor: cut out the preaching, friend, you're not on the Grand Mosque's minbar! Drunkenness has its good sides. I am an intern in the gastroenterology division of Mustapha Hospital, and I know whereof I speak. Drunkenness isn't as bad as you pretend. You mustn't make yourselves feel guilty for drinking, that only increases the bad secretions and provokes inflammatory allergies.

The witness, inspired: to get drunk only leads to disorder and discord, and he knew it. It is a preventive measure. The big powers use our drunkenness to fuck us over, and not only in Lebanon and Palestine, just see what is really happening and what they hide from us as if we were prepubescent boys. That's how come we get boozed up every day! He knew it, he did. The angels had cleaned his heart. ... Yes, sin and vice outweigh any usefulness. He knew the Arabs and their camel-driver ruses well. Didn't he say: *"There are a hundred kinds of evil, and the Arabs account for ninety-nine of them!"* Even uncle Hamza, Anthony Quinn, was not presentable! We do not merit our prophet's indulgence...

Someone else: Exactly! You said it! Yes, it's all an illusion. Gabbing gets you all excited. You no longer know how to stop. You blow up for no reason. Facts swell to inconceivable proportions. You get to where you confuse the rooster and the donkey under the table; you get to where you yourself do the animal with them and, in the end, you wind up puking in the morgue! Excess you deplore once you're sober again!

The neighbor, cocky: Oh come on, a little booze up is just the right thing to straighten out one's head! Don't look down on it. It is a kind of medical purge. The ancients knew its good use: *"ebriari semel in mense,"* that's Latin and is in fact prettily reworked by Ibn Sina in his poem on medicine:

Iyyâka an taskara tûla ad-dahri
wa in yakun famarratan fi ash-shari...

For that the virtues of wine are numerous and science discovers new ones each day.

The other: wow, man, you sure are an optimist! Truly. What a change from those follow-the-bread-ers and their belly button meditation sinecures.

The neighbor: you have to! Yes old friend, you absolutely have to! I followed the classical route, Latin and Greek, and I got my doctorate in Strasbourg and it's the moola that chases me. Oh, it wasn't all that easy, but I'm lucky. Can't complain, I have no major problems. Got a place to live. Unmarried, I am at home wherever I happen to be, but it is in this here galley that I like to get high. I don't overdo it, but I enjoy all of it, well, at least everything I can get ahold of. I follow the pleasure principle. Duty, first, of course, but the ludic is king! There are ways for the citizen to get high, don't believe appearances. This country isn't a private hunting ground, even if there are many barriers sporting "do not enter" signs. I won't let myself be discouraged. I support my biologist comrades who are doing cutting-edge research on the wing of the cockroach and others who are working on the sexuality of bees and I don't give a hoot about shiny rhetorical public speeches. Avoid at all cost leaving your balls in the cloakroom! I am fighting for quality social medicine, though propositions to open a private practice are not lacking, and know that private medicine will soon openly impose its legalization. I don't care! Truly, I don't give a shit! I regret that the League didn't notify me, a doctor is important indeed, but who knows me?... I'll try to get out of my anonymity. One just needs to be competent. And active. I must be an idealist, yes, that's what it is... If there's shit everywhere it must be because it suits a large majority of people; it can't be otherwise. There's no mystery! If I worry about it, it will kill me; that's how I am! So, what to do? I remain in the ideal, there at least I feel high. Of course I don't forget the fuel... Is there anything that's better? Whatever, I know what I don't want and what no one is going to make me swallow.

The other: oh, well! For someone educated you truly are an optimist, and that makes me feel younger, lemme tell you! You're really cool! I haven't studied as much as you have, but I'm no ignoramus, I watch television and I've messed with the antenna so I get Spain and the first French channel, and before the restrictions I had a subscription to *Science et Vie*. I've had great moments in my life. I still remember the taste of the pure butter madeleines, of the *mouna* and the *religieuses* at the *Café de la Genevoise* in the olden days. Lemme tell you, your optimism lifts my spirits and that's good. To think that I was despairing!

Someone: who cares about his jerk-off optimism! Me, I haven't read anything and I don't remember anything except that I want to drink!

The witness: madeleines, I like those too! If I'm not mistaken the French Embassy is situated on Madeleine Lane... I've gone there, it's a bit rural out there...

I, shouting myself hoarse: flush the countryside and the cakes and those memories that paralyze our asses down the toilet! A round, barkeep! The same, it's on me. And make it spurt through the heart!

The neighbor: I've got the faith, an unwavering faith. My heart is vast. I love Algiers among the sparks. I love the *nouba* in the bars of Algiers and the women of Algiers at the wheel of a car. I love it when there's jokes told around me and when we stuff ourselves with shrimp cooked in white wine in Fort-de-l'Eau or chez Sauveur. I love the lapidary poetry of obscene and blasphemous graffiti in the toilets of the Atlas. And I love, I love above all else when the people mischievously assumes its sovereignty, not the delegation of power, nor the neons' blinking:

BY THE PEOPLE AND FOR THE PEOPLE

... So there was this porter in Baghdad, who was out of work. This was in the days of the Abbassides and at a time of economic crisis and a politics of austerity. One day the unfortunate porter was peacefully walking past the golden palace of the caliph, dragging his cart full of fresh grass for his three rabbits, when the guards stop him. They are insulting and doing what they are there for. They scream: "It's forbidden to cut the grass... You papers! Your ass! You're just a poacher!... Bring your mother!... Scoundrel!" "I'm innocent! I haven't done anything! I don't have any of the things you're asking for, and no money to pay the fine," he moans. "If you want, I'll leave you my cart so you can use it to reinforce your armoured anti-Mongol divisions; as far as the grass is concerned, Vizier Dja'far who loves the stuff, can graze on it, it's first rate. And to you, have pity, I'll give my two rabbits, the only thing I own; they are cuddly, easily penetrated and have all the necessary know-how."

... The porter, after being nastily set upon, was thrown in jail while the captain of the guards hurried to tell the Commander of the Faithful of his insolence. "Bring that impudent porter immediately before me!" Harûn ar-Rashîd screamed. In the Council Room, ar-Rashîd sat majestically on his throne. And standing on his right was Ja'far the Barmekide and on his left Masrûr the executioner of sentences. All three had an angry countenance. The finely-honed triangle suspended in the air.

The porter was lying at their feet.

"So! Gummy-Eyes! Worm! Turd!" the caliph thundered while rolling his eyes to appear more terrible, "tell us your story, and make it fast!"

"I demand *aman*, immunity from punishment," the porter breathed. He added without getting flustered, having told himself that at the point he was, a show of audacity could not harm him more, "and some food, and then I'll listen and submit to your orders."

"I'll grant it," the caliph said, astonished by the man's nerve and by his own reaction, for he immediately sent the sword-carrier away and ordered a guest's meal to be served right then and there.

… The porter sat down on the floor having eaten his fill and calmly told the whole story, with slight exaggerations. The caliph burst out laughing though the vizier was fulminating. "It's in the bag!" our rascal thought.

Then ar-Rashîd grew somber, wondering what to do with this raggedy pro-letarian without loss of prestige, for among the Muslims he was seen to be evenhanded. The problem was difficult to resolve: having granted the *aman* and shared salt, he obviously could not act harshly. The other, who was smoothing his mustache, knew as much. He couldn't either send this simpleton back home, just like that, without any punishment, for that would be a redoubtable innovation, the kind that eventually caused the downfall of empires…

He had to make up his mind quickly. Get out of this situation honorably. Ar-Rashîd took an angry tone (he played the role): "You are either a son of a bitch or an adapt of hashish!" The porter came back at him immediately, with a slight bow: "Between the two, sir, I wouldn't spit on the ortolans."

And all of them (even the vizier) burst out laughing…

The other: ah! thank you, thank you. That's wonderful! You can't know how that fills my heart with pride, to meet young people like you who are patriots, happy, popular, optimistic. Not those naked eye moon watcher faces! Thanks. That's very good. Go on. It's a priceless dilation.

The voice from the back of the room: I need a drink, not stories! We want something liquid!

The waiter, vaulting over the bar: my hours are up. I got a bus to catch.

He, daydreaming: the Arabs!… Did they ever exist anywhere?… And the Arabian horse frolicking on the English lawns!

The witness: still, we need true values, stable values, a restoration of our-selves. Patience and good will, we're not monkeys!

The neighbor: God only knows!

The other: enough already with that quibbling, grunts are for dogs! I'm paying this round. Another round, waiter! At least that one the sharks won't get.

... Finally we all agreed.

Together: okay! One more!...

The drinkers' relaxation was an edifying spectacle for two future engineers, two neophytes touched by male inebriation and comically wobbly.

It had been a didactic session.

We had our entries at the cinematheque. The screenings took place in the morning, at ten o'clock sharp.

The cinematheque was the only establishment with an absolutely precise time table. At the beginning, the latecomers among the public had bitched, even threatened: they had tried to bring pressure to keep a certain elasticity; but eventually everyone submitted to the rhythm of the screenings. There were seven regular cinephiles. An adequate number for private jokes. We were serious buffs indeed. Always on time. Somewhat loony, but festive, and not in it for any profit. A bit crazed. Fans. Pioneers!

The projectionist, who had gotten his start before Independence as the usher of the Colisée theater where he had worked in tandem with a mute who unhappily died when the OAS blew up the movie house in the spring of '62, would project a random reel and take off to the corner café leaving us alone in the theater, where we'd spend the morning in semi-darkness reconstituting the film, shot by shot, controversy always lurking, each of us taking off from a given sequence, getting carried away by some miraculous draught of fishes, raving about a specific frame, extolling this or that camera movement or viciously exposing the invisible strings of a montage or the way in which a given effect was achieved.

That's what you call vice! It's like the worm squirming about inside the apple, with the result that no one can sit still. ... We never saw a movie from beginning to end. It wasn't worth it, it didn't lead anywhere, it was too long, in the end, a killer, made you drift off into distraction, a traffic jam for the eye. Trained as we were, a few minutes were enough to form a solid judgment. The kind of professionalism some newspaper critics were jealous of. There was always one of them who would come and, somewhat embarrassed, quiz us before writing his article. This was not a given: to find delight in joyfully decoding the hermetic message of olympians on a tightrope.

We treasured and cherished the credits, *fiat lux*, and left the place in a bad mood each time the usually old, mangled and routinely massacred copy, didn't include them, which happened often given the dilapidated condition of the badly maintained stock and the destruction wrought by the projectionists, those specialists of the random cut.

Our recriminations, our annoyed reclamations, even our petitions were unable to remedy the situation. Other priorities monopolized the minds. Contingencies hardened sensibilities. What does a trivial snip of the scissors matter!

…

The spectators know. They call censorship stealing. An example:
— Question of the one who wants to go in: "How's the movie?"
— Answer of the one coming out: "Not bad, but they steal much of it!"
(…THEY, the Pretenders, dilapidating the manor's reserves by throwing big feasts.) But the blacklist, overarching censorship, and discretionary power were something more than simple theft.

…

Among our group was the waiter of a cheap eatery on the rue de Tanger, LA SOUMMAM — specialties: fried bonito, squid and whiting. Brain and sole meunière. Sardine fish balls with rice. Grilled lamb testicles. Fish soufflés (made to order). Onion and parsley vinaigrettes, tchakchoukas.

His name was Mhand. At fifteen, as stowaway on a Norwegian tanker, he found himself in Vera Cruz. The Greek sailor who caught him in the hold said nothing to the captain ("We Algerians, we were well thought of!" Mhand said) and helped him get ashore. He had a hundred francs in his pocket. After having worked all over Mexico, Panama and El Salvador, he decided to cross the Rio Grande with some Mexican peasants who knew the route. To try one's luck … With the chunk of beeswax apportioned, dodging drifting in silence, eluding lady Fate. He settled in San Francisco, for a moment, as stevedore at the covered market, then in Los Angeles. Dishwasher, waiter, chauffeur, delivery man. The small jobs of the footloose. Contacts among the underworld, the streetwalkers, in show-biz; nothing major. Finally he landed a job as an extra in Hollywood, thanks to Hedy Lamarr whom he helped out one night on the ramp of a crosstown freeway. "Both her back tires were punctured and she didn't have a spare wheel," he would recount, "so I took her into my Chrysler. After a while she said to me, 'I am Hedy Lamar!' — 'A pleasure to meet you,' I answered, 'I am Mhand ould al-Hadj!' She started to laugh, certain that I was joking but I had not recognized her." It is she who introduced him to the movie people. "Business was good, everything was cool."

The young starlets were fighting over him. He had his pick.

He even stood in for Marlon Brando in *The Wild One!*

AMERICA!... MARIKAN... inconceivable!...

Then, one day, he dropped it all. There was no one he could have consulted with. It was in sixty-seven. He rushed back to Algiers: the American army wanted to draft him and send him straight to Vietnam.

He kept repeating, whenever he could: without boasting too much, I can say my case is special. I didn't visit the United States on fake business expenses! I was known there! I was a well-known gentleman over there, a *big man!* Ah, sonavabitch of a war! It ruined everything. I was American, but algerian Algerian, and we were the Viets. I wasn't gonna shoot at my people! I already have a maternal uncle who deserted to Indochina and has settled there. So, could you imagine me spilling the blood of my cousins? ... Wasn't I right to come back? I often ask myself if I didn't do something stupid. Where's my life? ...

We always waited in vain for his appearance in the movies in which he pretended to have been an intelligent walk-on...

He and I suspected him of being ever so lightly mythomaniac (clues: the discordance of time and events; the lying intonation of the voice; certain vaguenesses in the narration) but we would not contradict him. There were many mythomaniacs in Algiers.

We thought: "What's the point in getting bogged down in diatribes? And if he wasn't bluffing. Couldn't one think for once of something else than *one of those braggarts, one of those rogues this black earth nourishes so many of, craftsmen of lies one is unable to see through?* Deep down, it's his story, his history. That's how we knew him and took pleasure in his company. Why get involved in an investigation that would break the charm?…" We had always maintained that one had to leave everyone free to journey any which way…

Mhand would take us to his eatery, very often when his boss was absent, and would serve us beer in earthenware pots because the place, owned by a Kabyle hadj from the mountains, was the favorite meeting place of a clientele that was devout and devouring, nit-picking and satisfied by gilded koranic verses in relief in shiny simile-wood frames.

This was the age of swanky in-your-face piety. They vied with each other in showy devotions, dressed in the soberly ostentatious outfits with alluringly perfumed prayer beads that constitute Friday apparel. We pretended to ignore dress fashions, broadcasting into the fearful swish: *"I do not adore what you adore and you do not adore what I adore"*… There was neither evil nor artifice (impure intention) in the good-natured and healthy joviality with which we infringed upon what was forbidden according to certain, excruciatingly hairsplitting exegeses — the sin! Enough for eighty strokes of the whip, in terms of legal punishment, in the sitting position, and in the nude for males — and we continued to drink abundantly to our cinematographic critiques without in the least worrying about a hidden god, who, we were certain, would scorn fade-in fade-out dissolves, cinerama, relief, expensive reconstructions, Dolby-stereo sound and the delicate shadings beyond black-and-white. It was a climate conducive to various formalisms.

In fact, God never disturbed our debates, to my great disappointment. God was absent from all invocations. Flashes: a Great Manitou conveyor of buffaloes to the great prairies. An anonymous spectator, offering in hand. A silent sovereign on Olympus catching each audacious word. A director of the National Security in the process of dissecting his henchmen's reports. *"The one who holds the realm in his hands,"* life and death in test tubes… Fluid…

On one of the nights of the Decree, it was in September, we had organized a non-stop all-nighter. There were chicken sandwiches, pizzas and thermos flasks of coffee to keep us awake. All night long no strange and beneficial light, except that of the projector (a different kind of lightbulb), led us jubilantly to manifest the untangled inmost depths of our partially calcinated desires. The long night spent ingesting coffee and cold chicken in the dark room, the roof gaping, open to the stars, prey to illusory illuminations. (... Sole light, illuminating, it counts and accounts for a longevity at ease in the moment of its descent, yet ungraspable.)

Happiness, oh happiness, o mother of Augustine!

Once upon a time I'd fall asleep with the children of the neighborhood standing guard on the terraces, defying the curfew, the monstrous and humid darknesses, to grab the passing light and make a wish, and soursweet bonbons, chewy toffee, dark *Bambin* chocolate in apron pockets to console us of appointments missed through our fault. We had no handkerchiefs.

Certain looks perpetuate the wait.

Ears hammered by Sirhân's gallop, the mind feverish in the simoom, gambols, dazzled by forked lightning. The long-buried prayer: "O Mother-of-his-father implore the just spouse to appear..." "*O Eye of Mercy...*"

He confessed to me that he had stopped believing in God last summer after devouring Lautréamont's *Maldoror.*

I didn't dare give a verdict. Take the risk of the wrong bet.

... we were at ease in our skins and cinema was but an entertainment in the eyes of the people of the first prayer row, which is not the fifth row of those seated on the bench (in fetal position), impatient. You would prop yourself up in your seat to see well. You stretched out your legs avoiding the rivulets of spit and sperm. You would stuff your nostrils with jasmine to escape the stink of the fitted carpet.

And yet there were days when everything looked down to me, downright disgusting me. A cesspool! How could you live! I couldn't bear our gang of gay down-to-earthers any more.

We were pathetic, mediocre losers.

I would yell threateningly at whoever tried to approach me: leave me alone! Peace! Don't touch! I don't want to see anybody. Today I'm feeling down... "*I'm blue... I'll put my head on a railroad line...*"

It so happened that there were basically no railroad tracks to throw oneself across (despite the complaints of successive five-year plans). I was neither hungry nor thirsty and I didn't have a stereo system in front of which to get high behind my Ray-Bans.

Deep down inside I was railing: sweep it away! a broom! a broom stick! Ha!... may the moment finally come to leave like a god and venture among the blacks and feast facing hecatombs of bulls...

* * *

(…)

I wasn't dreaming. No, I wasn't dreaming at all. It was indeed a scorpion the size of a lobster. A yellow scorpion with brown highlights. It came at me in fits and starts. I gazed at it attentively, biting my lower lip. The monster! It became invisible every time I tried to draw its presence to the attention of my companions. It reappeared when I kept quiet. This way of behaving diminished its credibility in my eyes, but I had to face the facts because it came to a halt right besides my mattress and screeched as it raised itself up: tsee, tssseee, heh, tsee, why don't you and I sign a pact, okay? You say nothing to your buddies and I'll watch my step. No reason to get everyone involved in our *bizness*. Moreover I didn't abandon my fine blonde sand, my desert's sweetness, my darling silver oasis and all my dear kin just to make trouble in some Moorish bath. I'm not in any kind of need, you dig.

I thought, that takes the cake, a talking scorpion!

The scorpion: what's so surprising? Don't be surprised, God is great! I'm not just any old scorpion. Look at me carefully, I am a marabout of pure and noble extraction. Given natural selection, atmospheric pollution, and administrative redistricting, our race is on the road to extinction. In my family, we would imitate the white man. My first cousins have infiltrated the northern administrations and I have a sister who invests in travel agencies… That's giant, isn't it! But there's crazier to come: check yourself out closely in a mirror!

I thought: this is a provocation, if I ignore it, I'll lose face stupidly.

The scorpion: let me come to the point: I've heard you mentioned in the summer gatherings of the brotherhoods of the Ouled Naïl clans, highly laudatory talk, let me reassure you, and I wanted to be reassured, or to assure myself that you really existed. That's how I am: a pragmatist, a bit of a materialist, oh! just as much as needed; I like to verify everything myself. Now, it is said that you have a slight lisp, a beauty spot on your right cheek and elongated ear lobes; those are signs characteristic of someone predestined to perfect love. My grandfather taught me this before he died. I've also read it in one of Djaber's alchemical treatises. Tell me, is it true?

I thought: how low have I fallen! What a disaster! Here I am, reduced to listen to the b.s. of a base animal. This scorpion is putting me on. He is trying to con me for some unknown reason. Why don't the others notice anything?

The old fakir was still spouting his deafening prose and never stopped handing around blunt after blunt, I was squirming in my seat, prey to a growing restlessness. Again and again I nudged him with the elbow to no avail.

I thought it over: the phenomenon may be inexplicable but I just can't let myself be led by the nose by some verbose creepy crawler!

I came to a decision: damned well strike.

I took my slipper and slapped it down on the critter, on the side of the rubber sole. The slam made some jump up but didn't disturb the flow of the narration. All of them, with faded eyelids and in total concentration, were silent *"in reverential contemplation."*

The scorpion was twisting its tail. He was changing from copper to black-ish-brown. He defecated a stinking gelatinous mass that drenched him and from which he tried to extricate himself, sobbing. Eyes wide open, I accepted the hallucination, an uncompromising reality.

The scorpion: you are uncharitable, truly. Alas, I arrive from afar, dog-tired, for the pleasure of meeting you and conversing with you for a brief moment — for it is also said that you are a poet! — I had hoped to find a friend and you can think of nothing better to do than to crush me like I was some vulgar cockroach. Did I offend you? I didn't even ask you for the time of day! You see how you are? You really are a northerner! A little man!

I said to myself: no, I mustn't. I don't want to. I cannot tolerate familiarity with an animal. I do not want to demean myself. It is an insult to my station.

(I corrected myself: but was my station human? And I immediately rebelled against this idea because that was not something ever to be doubted. I was the Governor on this earth, that was me indeed. Nobody could question that.)

The scorpion: but the animal is you, you damn idiot! My ancestors didn't plough the stony earth. They looked up to the heavens and said: "We want to be like that!"

I thought: this is too much. If I let this go on, he'll think he can get away with anything; these animals, they don't know any limits. He is quite capable of getting me to talk to him! Of getting me to go and feast at his table! Oh Iblis, how justified was your arrogance! For this is what sophisms reduce men to — to be the equals of insects! Why bother with reason...

The scorpion, who wouldn't stop gabbing: listen, I've got a whole lot of questions to ask you and I think you are capable of answering them for me, now, it is said that passion is a fire that burns slowly but simmers for a long time, that snuffs the embers in the flesh like diaphanous pain...

Exasperated, I cracked a match and threw it on his back. I let out a sardonic ha, ha!, clapping my hands. I felt it sizzle. A little whiff of barbecue floated up.

I yelled: where's your rhetoric now?

The scorpion: what a dumb ass! Here you are, confined to the shadow of the night yet claim to be a man! Sad idiot! So uptight! Don't you see the sun kneeling at the seam of your jeans? And the dwelling, you think it's empty! Your loss. Your loss. You did not even question me about my country. You are so inhibited. And now you'll have my suicide on your conscience. I didn't want that, and I'll never forgive you! Not because of my life, for in my death I'll find another life, but because you are worthless! Go look at yourself!

He shoved his sting into his cephalothoraxes. I watched him burn and crackle.

... The animals come off best, I reflected. Make no mistake, those aren't just fables. There's truth in them. Thus the plenipotentiary donkey who had gone to the National Assembly to file an amendment concerning the unalienable rights of house pets and proposed a correction to the rules governing the hunt, that wasn't just a bar joke!...

I couldn't admit it. My education, what science I had, threw up barriers. Where I came from everything was possible, but not that! There were inviolable laws, inescapable principles, a philosophical reason, a religious order, a logic inside each one; there were mathematics! I trembled at the thought that maybe we were cut off from the rest of the world and ruled solely by the instinct for survival, the lower belly, and had jettisoned all traditional safeguards. The remainder of our insularity.

Incredible things were happening that our press passed over in silence, that we ourselves instinctively kept silent in our gatherings, and that we didn't know how to interpret quietly.

That the animals be burdened with our grievances, have pity!

Carbonized meatball, with an oily halo, there, at the foot of my bed, palpable proof. I smelled it.

from: *People of Mosta*

ULYSSES AMONG THE FUNDAMENTALISTS

He had opened the newspaper directly to the cultural page, the only section whose meager columns he liked to skim through. He found the national press to be a most distressing read; on top of which the ink used dirtied your fingers. He cried out when he saw the photo, put his trembling hand against his forehead. Putting the paper down on a clean corner of the table, he leaned over it to read the small inset signed APS. Silvana Mangano had died, the old one. His hurried reading yielded only this terrible bit of information which instantly plunged him into an abyss of melancholia. She — so beautiful to look at! "She is dead!" he mumbled...

There, amidst the chipped cup half full of *dirty* coffee in a ray of sunshine, surrounded by breadcrumbs, splatters of jam and the newspaper to the side, he couldn't imagine — he was as if anesthetized — the death of the actress. Could she disappear just like that? Without any supervening catastrophe upsetting the order of the day? The earth didn't open up. He looked around as if to make sure of it. The restaurant room seemed normal. The customers were quietly eating their breakfasts. He distractedly thought about the Americans who had bombs with double timing: they exploded above their targets forming a heavy cloud that could stay in place, remaining immobile for several days. A laser ray in the middle of the cloud then triggered a reaction that sucked all the oxygen out of the circumscribed space in a fraction of a second, snuffing all animal or vegetable life. They were being experimented. The scientists claimed that the programming was infallible. Destiny? Unlucky star? He expected no relief from the tears or the blood or the disguised voices...

The photo was a bad reproduction of a shot from *Bitter Rice*. Hmida had informed the gang of the meaning of the title: "Rice is like love, it is life itself; and the life of the poor ain't no cake." He pretended that bitterness was the salt of life. The women were laboring like the men to survive because the condition of the peasantry was so harsh. But there was Silvana Mangano! She was curvaceous and knew how to tantalize. They were all drooling, eyes fixed on the movie screen, even Dadi who was finishing the sixtieth section of the Quran and who was cutting sheikh Adda's classes to hang out with them. Benchâa, who was still going to the hammam with his mother, swore that he had seen Silvana Mangano's double and that he had brushed against her loincloth in the hot room.

His eyes wandered over the photo at great length while he stuttered vague mumblings. As his eyes managed to distinguish her, she brought back the excessive sensations of childhood. Despair and enthusiasm commingled as a strange stirring grew in his belly. The first pallid awakenings to the body's dampness, the excruciating cliché of a lost paradise, back there, at the seashore. The fearful parents forbade them to go swimming as long the marine genies had not slaked their ritual pedophile appetites by swallowing the seven ritual victims of summer in jubilation and in full view of the town's citizenry. "The sea is a carnivorous labyrinth," they would say. The Hamdawa brotherhood would sacrifice a black bull garlanded with red cloth and kauri shells; they would daub the reefs of Kharrouba with the still warm blood to entice *those people.*

Hmida had paid cash. Fifty douros to the *gimp,* the cashier at the *Cinélux,* to buy the photo of the actress in black stockings reclining on a barracks' bed. Has this unforgettable pose forever determined my erotic fantasies? How many times, strolling along a boulevard or down the alleys of some park, haven't I inadvertently stumbled across this memory!

The purchase of the photo had been quite an affair. Hmida was gifted for this kind of transaction! He made his money back in less than a week and made some extra on top of it, by having everyone shell out one douro for the right to keep it in their hands for three minutes behind the Bigord Mill. He was very careful that nobody should dirty the picture. We were fighting over our turns. A true potlatch for our gang… Finally, after many pleas and entreaties sweetened with assorted bits of *karantika* or paper cones of chick peas with cumin, he accepted to sell it to me for one *Blek le Roc* and one *Rodéo* comic book only after his business had started to fall off.

Hmida was the only one of our gang who had seen *Ulysses* with Kirk Douglas in the lead role, in Oran. That was after he had been released on probation from the juvenile detention center. His uncle had taken him to the *Murdjadjo,* an air-conditioned cinema with bar — his enticing descriptions of the place would leave us glum — after he had promised that he would not steal or run away and that he would study hard because the country would need educated people. He agreed to tell us the story of the movie, interlaced with his personal adventures, many of which were invented, evenings after school, against payment of a sandwich or a *crépone* or a contribution toward a movie ticket.

He told himself under his breath that nothing would be the same as before. That that period had been blessed and beautiful, all in all, a period of happiness. Yes, happiness! Despite the *implacability of colonialism!* What did that mean? A cumbersome stereotype. A part of his family had been decimated by the paras during *Operation Binoculars*. His father had spent his youth in jail; he had been tortured. He had embarked clandestinely for Marseilles to escape capital punishment and had settled in Nantes where he had found a job in a factory. After three months he gave up any idea of returning to Morocco. That's when he enrolled in a center for vocational training to learn a trade and started to organize the first FLN networks. Condemned to death by the MNA, he moved to Paris. His old friend from the PPA, Si Zitouni, who had stayed faithful to Messali, had warned him in time. Shortly thereafter Si Zitouni was executed. His father dropped politics and had his family join him.

He never understood his father's gesture. To have abandoned the struggle midway through seemed like an act of cowardliness to him, but at no moment did he manage to sort it out with him. He overheard many discussions in which old companions would side with his father and praised his integrity. He himself would just say: "I fought to the very end after my own manner, without asking anyone for anything. God be my witness."
...In the end, the final return — of which he had been dreaming so much it poisoned the life of his whole family — was made in a coffin...
He had a brother, nephews, nieces who today were French. While he, he was here. He wondered why. A strong dose of masochism. He did not want to leave this country where he was withering away. It was for this place that he felt concern. Something tugged at him deep inside. It also allowed him to bitch about everybody else and come off best. Elsewhere he was only a tourist, or worse: an exile...

Yes, an era of happiness... Maybe even exactly because of the colonial presence that forced them to take up the gauntlet. It was over. That era was dead. Like *l'Algérie de papa!* These times are past and what's yours is yours. We weren't able to make anything from it. It shrunk to nothing. What a waste! Ah! To grow old!... In these disconnected and painful episodes of a tragic history was there anything that could provide material for luminous chants for the coming generations? Time was drowning, parched owl fluttering above the chipped bowl.

He began to hate himself to have had to state such a banality as if he was afraid of the silence of his interlocutor. What's the point of having studied like a madman, without allotting a minute to fantasy, when it led to uttering such stupidities!

… He tore up the page and left the newspaper on the table.

He got late to the congress. The hall of the palace was buzzing with delegates commenting on an insulting caricature published that morning on the front page of the daily *Chaâb*. The Arab-language press was ferocious and viciously aggressive. She named *Parti de la France* — what a disgrace! — all those who aspired to the harmonious development of all the country's cultures or who demanded a bilingual, scientific and secular educational system. The most basic use of good sense was decried as a borrowing from a foreign mentality. One was on an alien planet. All were responsible, however. In an artificial one-upmanship… But the Arabs of yore, *those we hold dear,* not those flabby bellied ones standing guard under the harems' moucharabiahs, knew how to treat the digs, the sons of bitches and the viper tongues. They passed right in front, inflexible. Members of the police forces kept busy mulling around…

He ran into Smaïn in the cafeteria. They embraced. He liked Smaïn. They had known each other for a long time. Smaïn was an associate professor at the law school. He drank a lot in the bars opposite the courthouse and in the *Brasserie des facultés* in order to perpetuate a long gone student life. Drunkenness allowed him to give free rein to a suicidal humor, overflowing with warmth and perspicacity, which gave brilliance to his long digressions. He belonged to that rare category of novelists Nazim Hikmet speaks of. Though Smaïn was rather an alcoholized novelist, enamored of Saint-John Perse and Seferis. That's who he liked best. He spontaneously opened up to Smaïn in order to get a part of the weight that was depressing him off his chest.

"Silvana Mangano died! And here we are, bored stupid in this sinister place while a whole part of our childhood, its most luminous bits, vanishes. Do you realize what that means? You don't even know who Silvana Mangano is, I bet! How have you been able to live? Ah, you can't understand the shock this news has caused! It isn't only her death…"

He told Smaïn, who never had enough time to go to the movies, the beautiful dream of love — no one in the gang could really explain what that meant — that Silvana Mangano personified. He described her enchanting metamorphoses in the film. She incarnated both Circe and Calypso: the lover who keeps Ulysses in her magic cave by making him drink a philter that will make him forget his homeland. When one loves, nothing else exists anymore; from being futile one becomes serious, grave. You learn that in all movies. The wand eliminates the too cumbersome companions. The seduced hero lounges in a sort of zoological garden without bothering about the animals that are trying to cuddle with him all the time. But conjugal love triumphs on the screen, that's Hollywood's morals! Also those of old Homer: he needed to reassure his audience so as to get his salary. There's Penelope in Ithaca. She waits faithfully and it is always her. The film director had found the trick to insinuate that Ulysses only left the witch to find her again at home; that he couldn't detach himself from her after having known her. She becomes the modest woman, the ideal one, for eyes addicted to idols. She was blonde and brown, totally fascinating! The unslaked burn. After the eclipse, she reappears in the role of Jocasta, again beautiful under the makeup. The character's obviousness produced a cathartic effect which the movie maker had sensed. She was luminous and lunar! Silvana Mangano! How feverishly he had waited for her, at each missed rendezvous, so as to forget the snow of the *rue de Froidevaux* in the night's depth.

Emotions were durable.

"You watch too many movies," said Smaïn.

In the afternoon, after they had finished reading the report on morality, he discreetly left the conference to walk down to the beach. He knew well that the congress was important — a historic moment! — that his presence meant a lot; he was not only there as a symbol or representation. "How to get out of this, given the context?" Smaïn had asked him brandishing the invitation. Yet Smaïn was less engaged than he was. This was the first public demonstration after years of clandestinity. He had put up with and supported this party through many difficult moments. And now he could no longer put up with these speeches. Wind! In private discussions he admitted that his attitude may shock certain of his friends; it was however of no consequence as far as the political situation was concerned. You couldn't hope for anything from anybody. He had never thought that he was indispensable and felt certain that on that count he was right. So much needed to be done in so many domains and there were so few means. So little time, too. You had to take the maximum of the latter in order to live. He scoffed at his own lamentations, felt them to be fake too. What was all this? A masked ball! How to penetrate souls? Answer the questions? Deliver oneself. Be in peace. Impressions of his adolescent readings of Tolstoy swam to the surface. The shepherds use a lash to drive the flocks to pasture. The world remained an indecipherable enigma and yet in bowshot distance. How to realize such a displacement? Remember:

> For in the past I was young man and young girl
> And bush and bird and mute fish of the sea.

Today all exits are blocked off.

On the promenade he made mental notes in order to make the brilliance of the day manifest and fix it in his memory more securely than by writing: "Superb weather!" "What a drought" "Summer persists, o ochre season, Happiness." "Tranquility, a crystalline space." "Gull time." "Aquatic fervor, sweat." "Alone, a siren…" "The sea sings" "The long legs satin-sheened in the black marvel of the stockings and love on the run sets fire to the austere dwellings of the tribe" "For long, the obscure blemish" "The line is pure when I bend over" "An ancient desire bursts forth… On the Cape, Ulysses wept. Ithaca evil. Each day sitting in the same spot as if immortality had no price. During the month of June, the scents of cedar and thuja are stifling. The crows and gulls were screaming above his head; their idiotic whirling amplified his misery. The soul stirs, then founders in a raw light that refracts the memories. Stomach contractions followed by burns. The body winds up going numb. In the cave the soft, algae-scented shadow permeated the atmosphere with gloom. Calypso couldn't understand a mortal's melancholy and the companions were dead. Ulysses was alone on this comfortable island where nothing happened that hadn't already been deliberated by the assembly of the gods…" He exalted himself. The images grabbed him. Inspiration.

"What am I trying to do?" he asked himself, embarrassed. And exclaimed: "No need for that! Artifice dulls the soul."

He took his shoes off. To go downstairs careful not to step on the shards of glass. He went and leaned back in the shadow of the parapet's small wall, facing the sea. To stay like that, for a long moment, eyes half-closed, settled in a vacuity he cherished. There was a slight swaying motion of the waves which faded away into the pause. Forget Achilles! … Nobody was going to come here to disturb him. This idea filled him with joy. He felt good. He breathed in deeply, delighting in the rush of air that excited his body from the inside.

The daydream's whims or the mischievous flight of the gulls made him regret the absence of Nausicaa and her companions. The ingenuous grace of their silhouettes naked for the bath. "It's not that long ago that they were there, playing ball, singing hymns to love," he thought sadly. The young girls remained cloistered according to the pseudo-modernist interpretation of the Law. The island was given over to dyed-in-the-wool masturbators, skilled in the art of marking the cards. The masters of the game. The pimps of the hour. The pretenders! The suitors! Good-bye to the shawl and the shimmering tunic and the golden flask filled with sun oil and the playful escort of nymphs, they would invite you to bathe in the current.

... He rose to his feet. He undressed. Earlier, when he had arrived, he had noticed the twisted sign at the edge of the road:

CROSSED OUT SWIMMING TRUNKS IN A RED CIRCLE.

He weighed down his clothes with a piece of perpend he found there. He breathed deeply. Then he rushed for the sea while beating his chest and uttering Tarzan's war cry.

...That's how the whole Suiza gang dove into water...

Come to where he didn't have footing any longer, he turned around and swam on his back while examining the shore. The water was pleasant. Warm for the season. He dove, trying to stay underwater for as long as possible. He had been a diving champion once, but cigarettes had taken their toll. He came up coughing. He floated on his back to rest. Then he began to imitate the dolphin's swimming style. Suddenly, he reared up. He pulled off his trunks and threw them across the waves. He burst out laughing — a long, loud laughter that made him swallow water — remembering how, way back, when they pulled their trunks off in the middle of the sea and put them on their heads better to complete the passage from the *Fantom Rock* to the *Salamander,* Zerrouki the Short was worried that the fish would nibble on his little whistle.

NECROLOGY

I was wet to the bone when I entered Allal's office in the *Maison de la Presse.* He was alone, busy wading through thick folders stacked on a table strewn with cigarette butts and newspaper clippings.

"Did you see the news?" I yelled, breathlessly.

"What news? You're white as a sheet and dripping. Sit down, relax. Dry yourself. Catch your breath. What's put you in such a state? Madame Gascar no longer terrorizes the citizenry of Algiers!"

"Othman B. just died. *Alger-Rép.* printed his obituary this morning. I'm shattered."

Allal stood up calmly and smiled, patting my shoulder.

"Algiers is still holding out! It is not our *Ottoman,* it's a homonym. I checked it out, as you can imagine! He is a tough old bird and the day when Azrael will put him to the question hasn't dawned yet! Come on, sit down. The coffee in the thermos is still hot; help yourself."

I collapsed on the rickety stool.

"Ahhh! His baraka holds!"

Othman B. was an old mujahideen who had been active in the Algerian Communist party and had enrolled in the International Brigades. He had known Duclos and the Pasionaria very well and claimed to have been the model for one of the characters in Malraux's *Hope.* In his old days he had become a bigot, thinking it normal to do so. "Communist, of course, but also Muslim; one doesn't renounce one's roots because of one's political stance. The Party is a single, unique leaven, but flour is not necessarily white!" he would proclaim. He had gone on the Hajj, in order "to see the place — Mecca and Medina are two superb tourist spots," as he would say every time he told the story of his trip, though he remained faithful to the Party that had taught him how to read. He belonged to that inflexible race of old ones. I appreciated his verve and old-time pontificating stance. He adored counseling the young, knowing full well that it didn't have much effect. I nearly systematically did the exact opposite of what he recommended, but I much enjoyed listening to him hold forth. He had, however, a lot of flair in his political analyses — which he didn't develop in front of everybody. He hated misunderstandings, groundless accusations and people who put words into his mouth. The mention of his name in the newspaper's obit section had been a shock to me... I began to relax...

"Do you know that that happened to me?" Allal said to me.

"What?"

"To be declared dead in the newspaper! I was in Paris, a year before the revolution started, busy setting up meetings between groups of French and Algerian intellectuals to discuss the question of nationhood. There were few of us in those days and of all sort of backgrounds. Not many communists! But that's the way it was... One morning a comrade from the CGT comes up to me and says, amazed: "You, you're not dead?!" I thought he was joking. I played along: "Guess I am!"

"I'm serious," he said vehemently. "Here, look at today's *Humanité*: *Allal M., a typesetter from Mostaganem, was thrown off his bicycle by a hit and run driver. The accident happened last night around 7 p.m. on rue Laffitte. The cyclist died from a brain hemorrhage...* You can understand my surprise when I saw you here"... Of course, it could have been me. Same identity; same profession; even the bicycle! I don't know if the guy was a homonym or if he had false papers in my name, and if so, how he had gotten them. Still, many comrades did believe I was dead that day! ... We raised many glasses to my resurrection *Chez Roger.*"

"Did you keep the newspaper?"

"Unhappily no. I can't even remember the exact date."

"You always have extraordinary stories to recount. I didn't know there were Franco-Algerian networks before the war. You lived through historic moments that haven't been written about anywhere. Why don't you write a book on that period?"

"How can you know? For thirty years now they have been misrepresenting history and hiding the truth. The basis for all that is anticommunism! Don't think I'm laying a Stalinist trip on you. You know, I remember very well, there was one guy in the group — a cynical and twisted bastard who has had quite a career since then — who kept repeating to me: 'When we'll have the power, we will eliminate you. We don't need your atheist ideology to make sure of the support of the masses. We have social Islam to motivate them. I remember the phrase. And that guy is one of the system's bigwigs. You see, what's happening is not happening by chance. It's been carefully prepared for a long time. One has to establish the itineraries and the biographies of each one of them to understand the process. It isn't via spontaneous generation that terror is being spread!"

"You should write all that down!"

"When? I don't have a minute for myself. And beyond that, we have to act. There's more work than I know how to handle. Maybe when I take retirement, maybe… But only if I have my daily pastis… writing makes thirsty!…"

"And you say that! All the people like you say the same thing. You remain tight as clams. I can't understand why this should be so. Meanwhile, whole pans of our memory are getting lost."

"Many of my generation have become camels!… Listen, you who are young. Open your ears wide and remember what you are told. And learn to tell a story. You know, one mustn't dramatize… A people never forgets what's essential to its being. No people can be fooled all the time! Memory is a very complicated thing. In fact, nothing really ever is lost. Memory works in the shadows. It loves secrecy. Apparent forgetfulness is its refuge during hard times. It waits for its hour to come and though the stomach rumbles it does not stop digging. There isn't only what's written down that remains. Spoken words also leave traces."

"I'm skeptical. It's the same for Othman B., nobody has bothered to collect his memories. A life of that order!"

"That's true. But scraps of his life perpetuate themselves in those who have known him; they meander and fructify at their own speed and will. It's life that is in charge of transmitting what is worth perpetuating. It keeps all the secrets. And does so better than any book, believe you me… Come, let's go check the archives, you can't hang about too long."

Allal introduced me to the newspaper archivist and before leaving me to my registers we agreed that I'd pick him up at six.

It was still raining. A dense rain that transformed the gutters into muddy torrents. It took skillful gymnastics to reach the Bar du Progrès. An inside as dreary as the outside. A rancid grayness grabbed you by the throat as soon as you came through the door; it slyly sucked you in and before you had the time to turn heel and flee it left you dizzy and incapable of extricating yourself from the mass of customers ensconced in the room's hubbub. I always let myself get caught despite my reluctance and the efforts I made outside, as if the stench of the bars of Algiers were reeling me in.

… Hamid motioned to us from a nook of the bar.

"He is well organized," I murmured.

We came closer. The owner took the tops off two bottles of beer without asking us what we wanted. He grabbed a crate and put it aside, motioning that it was reserved for us.

"I just came from the hospital," Hamid said. "Si L'Hoçine is in bad shape."

"Then we'll drink to his health. Nothing else we can do," said Allal with grave solemnity. And turning toward me: "Si L'Hoçine is an early member of the Federation of France. Hey, he reminds me of another obit in the paper: Antar! Do you remember Antar, Hamid? It was his nickname because he looked like Serrag Mounir. You can't understand if you don't know the Egyptian movies from those days… Antar had kept company with the circle of intellectuals before the war but, given that deep down he was a Messalist, he opted for the MNA. Once, I was with Yacine, we walk into a bar near rue de la Convention. We just happened to be in the area and didn't know anybody around there. You should have seen how all those guys got up and surrounded us! They were all MNA guys. Built like ice boxes. They took us for spies from the FLN. It gave us the jitters. Especially me. Yacine didn't give a shit. He was thirsty and didn't notice a thing. When he was loaded he would always hum the refrain of a song that Ali, an old immigrant from Sétif who worked as a fitter for Peugeot, used to sing to us in the hostel on rue Château-des-Rentiers. I still remember it:

> Shake, shake oh you girls
> May God turn you to ashes
> Georgette has set fire to my heart
> She, the girl from France…

That's what saved us… A guy comes rushing out of the back room toward us. It's Antar! He had recognized Yacine's voice. We had stayed friends. He embraces us and tells the owner: 'These guys, you'll serve them what they want. No alcohol restrictions and they don't pay. They're at home here!'… We never went back to his bar!… On another occasion Yacine was completely drunk when MNA assassins corner him on rue du

Four. They want to execute him because they apply the same directives when it comes to alcohol. By chance, Antar came by at that moment. One could have thought that he was our guardian angel. 'Watch out, that one you do not touch! He's precious. Look at him closely. You don't harm a hair on his head, got it! Don't touch him, he can do whatever he wants to do — he is our poet!' he told them straight out. Antar was the head of the MNA assassins in Paris and his guys obeyed his every word without questioning. In earlier times, Yacine had taken Antar to the theater of the Vieux-Colombier, had lent him books and given him his manuscripts to read. Antar always kept a soft spot for him, despite their political differences. To understand the guy's psychology you have to see that for him friendship always came before politics. Si L'Hoçine was a childhood friend of Antar's. The Organization, as we said in those days, had sent him to Mulhouse to set up networks. That whole region was controlled by the MNA — it was impossible to infiltrate. But Si L'Hoçine was unafraid. He was strong and didn't doubt the correctness of the FLN's positions. He goes to two or three cafés to check out the situation. The guys from the MNA find out. They kidnap him in his hotel room and drag him in front of their bosses. At the same time Antar was there to supervise the groups. As soon as he sees Si L'Hoçine he orders him to be released and let's him circulate and do as he wishes. That's how come Si L'Hoçine was able to recruit for the FLN throughout Alsace. The guys from the MNA must have thought that he was one of their moles; weird, isn't it? To get back to the story of the deceased, one day I'm reading in *Le Parisien* or *Le Monde,* can't remember in which one, that Antar has been executed by unknowns on rue Galande. The newspaper was talking about the rivalry between the MNA and the FLN for control over the Franco-Muslim population in France and mentioned a number of bloody settlings of scores. The article was very well documented! When I meet Antar's brother, I present my condolences while indicating that the FLN was justified in killing him. Guys like Antar represented a real danger for the Revolution. We couldn't afford the luxury of internal dissensions. I told him all that very naively, having a sense that he was not involved in politics. He agreed to several of my points by nodding his head. I tell the story to Si L'Hoçine who says to me: 'You are crazy! Antar was the assassin in chief of the MNA, but the executor was his brother. Why did you say those things to him...' Antar's brother knew that Antar and I were friends and because of that he thought well of me. One day — I've never understood why he did that — he comes to see me at the door of the printshop and confides to me: 'You know, Antar is not dead. He is in the Fresnes jail. The whole thing was orchestrated by the prefecture.' It's true that the MNA worked with the cops. Especially the last years. It will be necessary to investigate those matters one of these days… That's gonna hurt!… Well, some two months after the announcement of his death, I crossed paths with Antar on rue Scribe, near Opéra. He had two bodyguards and death in his eyes. He embraced me and asked for news of Yacine. I was scared shitless to be seen with him or that someone was posted in the neighborhood to take him out and me at the same time. I'll never forget his look. Death in his eyes! It makes me shiver just to talk about it… He was shot down shortly afterward in Bobigny."

"You should write it all down. You don't have the right to keep silent about all this. It's part of our patrimony. And on top of it all, it would help us understand those events. Today we feel so completely lost."

"I don't even know why I'm telling this story. I don't like it when it rains on this town. Come on, let's have another one."

from: *Moses' Fish*

... It was not far from Peshawar, in a stony wasteland surrounded by barbed wire. The camp had been organized hastily: a few barracks and prefab hangars set up according to a rectilinear plan: a vast circular space leveled and marked with lights serving as site for assembly and maneuvers, and as landing spot for the helicopters of the Pakistani army in charge of supplies.

The decor's flatness adds to the place's banality. Which gives an impression of desolation, accented by the rather vague route of the only access road, bordered with old utility poles — more like a bumpy trek, barely suitable for cars — that links the camp to the town.

The non-place dismissed from the travel stories where you are afraid of bumping into the Dry Tree at any moment.

(For a long time I was upset by the implacable atony of military structures... The buildings are packed down as if waiting for or wanting a metamorphosis.

Wherever the place may be, the landscape is systematically erased.

Maybe this is in fact nothing else than a camouflage technique to avoid the possibility of any trace being spotted.)

...

It has not been easy to regroup all of the Maghribian veterans of the Afghanistan war. Some of them had themselves adopted by the rebel tribes that had welcomed them. There they founded homes that they don't want to leave for anything in the world. Others, suspicious or dissatisfied with the absence of solid remuneration, prefer to keep fighting in the maquis with the dissidents of the resistance.

Their exist several rival factions, each with its own networks, its underground logistics, its occult financiers, its dearly acquired territories. Nebulae on the look-out. Newcomers are still flooding in, and in order to maintain discipline, they are still given training at the border.

This camp serves to make the inventory of all the strangers, old voluntary recruits, before they are repatriated to their countries of origin, or, as they case may be, before they get new postings.

Life in camp, monotonous and regulated, doesn't differ from that in a normal military barracks. Nothing exciting for this now demobilized and heteroclite bunch of young dropouts. Many had signed up from a taste of adventure and a fascination with a religion that promised them a sense of dignity. The recruiters had exalted the well-endowed garden promised to martyrs, good pay at the end of their period of service, and the exciting life of which they all dreamed amidst the parking lots of their overcrowded projects. They, however, had requested primarily respect and recognition in the depth of their being, a request stifled by their own sense of lacking any usefulness. They were inhabited by a despair so profound that only violent hatred could temporarily appease its bitterness. Jihad had been the royal path to bring them out of their idleness or their little con schemes.

Among the older ones the Algerians were the most numerous and, true to their reputation, the rowdiest. Rumor has it that those who go back home are immediately arrested and thrown into jail or sent to concentration camps in the Sahara where they are left to die from dehydration. The rumor, having magnified, engendered a hidden tension. A state that makes most of them anxious, irritable, and quarrelsome. So much had been promised to them, and now they felt betrayed. Some of them were discouraged and depressed from stewing in the uncertainty of their fate. They keep sending out teary letters of appeal, addressed directly to the President of the State High Committee, asking to be allowed to see their parents again. They swear that they are ready to make amends and to return to a normal life, as long as they are permitted to return home without being mistreated. But many, far from considering their enlistment as a youthful error in need of reparation, are eager to reenlist for Bosnia or any other cause where they can make use of their combat experience.

From time to time, fights break out. They reveal ancestral racial antipathies and profound religious divergences between the nationalities: the Sudanese believe in the imminent arrival of the Predestined One who will rid the world of all its ills; they share this belief with the Algerians and the Moroccans. The Egyptians blame the Iranian Revolution for folding in on itself rather than stimulating all the Parties of God in the world. The Chinese want to abolish birth control and return to polygyny without however breaking with Maoist collectivism. The Turks hope to reestablish the caliphate in Istanbul, and to federate the different peoples of Islam under their authority. The Tunisians lean more towards an Islamic republic directed by an assembly of men of letters from the small bourgeoisie. The

Yemenis and the Malians find that the tribal system is a better guarantor of the rights of the individual because it avoids the suicidal excesses of individualism. The Indonesians criticize the hegemony of the Arabs, and the Uzbeks and Albanians join the Chechens in their sharp critique of the doctrinal positions of Ibn Taymiyya. As far as they are concerned, the young immigrants dream of Islamizing their neighborhood in order to become its omnipotent emir. Under their regulation tunics they wear t-shirts with the head of Malcolm X and know whole sections of his incendiary speeches attacking the United States by heart.

However, a new current is transcending the ethnic divides, assembling them under the firm rule of theologians who proclaim themselves to be reformists. The principle that underlies this doctrine is the concordance between science and prophecy. From this simple dogma follows a categorical refusal of any *mystical drift* — those are the very terms of the most savant professors — in the reading of the Qur'an. There is only positivist comprehension, and thus the revelation is scientific. This tendency attracts the fanatics and the doctrinaires, those for whom the *mother of the Book* contains from all eternity the story of the world the opacity of whose woof and weft for human understanding is but the fruit of hazardous conjectures and of man's inability to open his heart to the evidence of the signs, those luminous milestones of the Message.

Certain temperaments are particularly high strung. The smallest pretext is good to start a brawl. A group of Kabyles, very assiduous students of the theology, are especially excited and vengeful. Its members exhibit an air of ferocious haughtiness. They pretend to be the only ones able to correctly interpret the sacred text. Because of them the camp has known murderous pitched battles on many occasions. The sight of blood stirs in them the male ferocity of the link.

Ken, the American instructor, and Sharif Shah, the Pakistani in charge of the camp, often intervene. They have trouble restraining the deep rivalries that divide them.

Mourad tells himself that maybe, in the fashion of ancient Rome, the American and Pakistani secret services don't see such happenings unfavorably and that they covertly encourage them.

...

They meet up in the dark of night, tossed about in a panicky to and fro. A monstrous fracas. The darkness is total. The generators have most certainly been sabotaged before the attack. Small groups dispersed within the camp exchange fire with submachine guns, machine guns, and automatic rifles. Blind, nourished and random fire that seem to obey no command. A waste of munitions. It's bedlam, a free for all. Macabre pandemonium. The screams of the wounded mingle with insults and injunctions yelled through the darkness. Great confusion reigns around the barracks and in the courtyard. A tracer bullet lights up the area. Mourad is blinded, but then, instantly adjusting to the light, makes out the gang of aggressors by the dining hall, scrambling like crabs on the shores of Canastel in moonshine. "They are playing at war, the idiots!" Mourad tells himself, retching. Suddenly he sneezes. With him, sneezing is a sort of alarm mechanism. He has barely the time to throw himself flat on the earth when a rocket blows the lateral barracks to smithereens. The air is thick with the stink of powder, blood, and sweat. The putrid and exciting odor of death! "Invariably equal to itself," Mourad thinks, disgusted. "And yet, tonight's fights are just tomfooleries!" Snorting, he gets back up on his feet.

The helicopter floods the camp with lights. It flies over the barracks, its projectors focused on the perimeter where the skirmish is happening.

Suddenly an authoritative voice comes through a megaphone, cutting through the chaotic cacophony. It sounded like the crackle of a piece of machinery beating down on an amphitheater, assailing every hidden nook and cranny as if refracted by the luminous circle. It calls for a cease-fire: "This is Ken speaking, this is your instructor speaking. Stop firing! Fucking shit! Stop fire! Stop your fucking crap! Go immediately back to your quarters. Do it now!"

Salvos and volleys redoubled in intensity, accompanied by the broadside of insults, as if the combatants wanted to give the finger to that voice and conspicuously and audibly flaunt their disdain for military discipline. They don't like to be called to order like conscripts. They all saw themselves as autonomous rebels, accountable only to their own organization. They didn't enlist in any kind of foreign legion but have come to fight as free men, as mujahideen, something they insist on constantly.

…The shots slowly fade out. Boys, half dressed, alarm visible on their faces, come out in compact bunches from their various barracks. They take off in all directions to go help the victims who are squirming on the ground calling for help. Electric torches are being used to move about the dark camp. Moans and calls tear the air, permitting the rescuers to orient themselves.

Mourad and Hasni join the general throng.

The helicopter pivots on its axis and goes to set down a bit further along on the parade grounds. Ken alights, megaphone in one hand, PA system in the other.

By the sentry box at the camp's gate, Mourad stumbles over a curled up body that moans in response. He kneels and gently takes it in his arms. He recognizes Laredj, a buddy from the maquis. He tenses, stammers: "Laredj! You okay!"

The man is clearly in bad shape. He mumbles in a barely audible voice: "They got me, the traitors. I'm losing all my blood. They are completely crazy, Mourad. Those cretins!" He grasps Mourad's collar, staring at him with bulging eyes: "It hurts a lot. I don't want to die here. I want to see Tigditt again. I've always hated Mosta but I want to die back there. Don't leave me here. Hold my index finger, Mourad, and recite the profession of faith with me; it's the end."

Mourad tries to reassure him: "Don't worry, they will take care of you. The camp is well equipped." He has spoken without thinking, while holding his index finger pointed at the sky. Over his shoulder, Hasni adds gaily: "You have great days ahead of you in Algeria. Soon you'll hasten to the *Es-Sunna* mosque in Bab el Oued to say your prayers. Have confidence!"

Laredj has closed his eyes. He no longer listens. He sees himself as a child on the threshold of Sidi Bessenoussi during the distribution of the semolina cakes. What a crush to get a piece! He was always afraid that the bas-relief lion's head on the lintel of the entry door to the mausoleum would suddenly come to life and leap at him. It is said that this happened just before the floods of the Aïn Sefra river. All night long the lion had roared in the streets of Tigditt, in the quarries and the lower Suika, forcing the inhabitants to flee their ramshackle houses to seek refuge in the higher parts of the town; this had saved them from drowning. Would Sidi Bessenoussi intercede for him on the Day of the Resurrection? Why does he remember this twaddle from his childhood today? The saints do not exist! He will have to face God without any intercessor. He has admitted the principle of this solitary responsibility since the day Fellouh recruited him into the ranks of the *Islamic Mission* in Tigditt. However, he doesn't want to be buried anywhere else than there, in Tigditt. The earth of the grave will be less heavy and he will surely have a respite before Judgment Day.

Mourad turns to Hasni and says: "Give me a hand, we'll take him back to the infirmary."

Laredj starts to moan: "No, no, leave me here; I can't move. It's too late. Promise that you'll have my body repatriated to Mostaganem. I want to be buried facing the sea. Swear that you'll do what it takes. I entrust you with the corpse. There is no God but God…"

A tall guy, with a face sharp as a knife's blade, in his fifties and wearing an impeccable navy uniform, approaches them, out of breath. Ken sweats large drops. He bends over the dying man. "Where is the camp doctor? What a mess!" His voice is hoarse. He now turns toward a Pakistani wearing a tightly fitting officer's uniform, a thin mustache, a green beret, all very British in style, and tells him: "Sharif, go check out barracks #3 and check that the imam is not in on all this, please. This time, it's gone too far!" The man called Sharif obeys without a word. Ken quickly walks from one wounded man to the next mumbling under his breath and nervously tapping his thigh with his megaphone.

"I'm going to get the doctor, Hasni whispers to Mourad and bends down over Laredj: Hang in there, old buddy!"

Hasni runs to the infirmary. Ken screams orders into the megaphone: "General assembly in the dining hall in one hour!" At the same moment the miradors blink and the light comes back on in the camp. Grinding his teeth he says to himself: " Will have to tighten the screws on these sons of bitches!"

(...)

Léa says: "You used to like lemon chicken, right? Unless your culinary tastes changed among the Afghanis. At times there are metamorphoses that make you want to crack up."

Léa and Mourad are lounging on shiny cushions right on the wooden floor. They eat facing each other. Relaxed. And yet, Léa's remark seems tinged with a reproach. Mourad asks himself if between them there will ever be anything else than this latent accusation of having dropped the other for no good reason. It locks him into a culpability he cannot get rid off. Now that he is getting ready to leave for far away, he would so much love for their relationship to cool down and flower into friendship. What keeps them from reconciling themselves? Deep inside, he is scared to investigate the question in more detail. The most difficult is past... "Call her!" Yves had said. "I don't know what her reaction will be, but it would be better to do it." He had mumbled vaguely: "I have to call her, of course!" He wasn't so sure about it, however. How to convince himself.

He had called her from inside the Jussieu metro station. She had been flabbergasted. This was an expression she loved to use to express her astonishment. Once over the surprise, her reaction had been strangely calm. A sequence of questions without fracas or animosity. He had feared the worst. "Listen, Léa, we can't speak of this over the phone... Okay... Tomorrow morning at 9 a.m. in the Balzar... Yes, yes, I'll be there for certain! It was a pleasure hearing your voice, Léa... Bye now... Yes, tomorrow..."

He had felt relief, as if swathed in water and heat, and then was totally overwhelmed once he had hung up. The old terrors he had thought he had overcome once and for all were slowly stirring again way down inside him, getting ready to resurface. Clouds were accumulating without having specifically been foreseen. Bad premonitions?

She had arrived late. More than a quarter of an hour late. He had a recollection of her intransigent punctuality. She never waited more than five minutes beyond the appointed time. "I hate to be left hanging!" she would say. Had she wanted to put him to the test? That was not her style. Maybe a last minute hesitation. Nothing forced her to come. He couldn't help expressing in thought the opposite of what he really thought. His mind found pleasure in injecting himself with doubt, in small increments. He did however wind up worrying so much that he bit his nails to the quick...

She was here. He had known all along that she would come. He had been certain of this despite his worrying. She had said "Good morning," but didn't hold out her hand or her cheek. She sat down without as much as a glance at him. As if she had sat down before an unknown client! The way she knew how to create distance so naturally always blew him away. He felt a draft of air sweeping against him. A sudden shiver made him bend over and submit inwardly. He squeezed his legs tightly together.

The silence had lasted a long time. A weightless silence. As if time was suspended. Asking himself how to break this tension without creating a fuss. Be patient, curl up in your shell and contain your emotion. He was moved. More than he thought possible, or more than he would have liked to be, maybe...

In a low voice: "I have never understood why you didn't come back from Birmingham after your training course." She was there, in front of him, sitting stiffly on the wall seat. Somewhat stiffly. Still beautiful to look at, in her sky blue suit, despite features slightly marked by fatigue and alcohol. Automatically: "She's aged!" Ashamed, he immediately thought better of it. He asked himself if she wasn't thinking the same about him. Certainly. Hadn't she scrutinized him meticulously just a moment ago, without batting an eyelid? He had felt the ice of her glance slide over him. It had made his flesh creep. Her gaze always managed to pierce him. Inevitably.

Years had passed, but nothing had moved. Everything was but ruins without resonance. What misfortune! He had learned how to bear it all, however. Be patient. To bemoan one's fate is of no use when the trace is emptying itself. What was he expecting? Why had he gotten in touch with her? She had come. After all, that was logical.

Did he feel pleasure at seeing her? His feelings were mixed. He didn't feel obliged to stay or meekly put up with her diatribes. — "A woman speaks to me like that, I'll slap her face!" he said to himself to show off, to flaunt a touchy masculinity — but had no intention whatsoever of walking out on her. He watched her on the sly.

Her long, Venetian blonde hair fell in curls on her shoulders. Which reassured him. "It's a good sign that she hasn't cut them." Maybe she had done so and they had already grown out again. One day when they had

had a vicious row she had cut them. He couldn't remember what the row had been about. They were fighting all the time. They'd patch things up very quickly. An epidermic magnetism inexorably drew them together again. The rows exacerbated their desire for each other. Considerably so. They both dreaded their bodies' reaction — a hungry ardor.

This time it must have been more serious. Without warning she grabbed the kitchen scissors and snap! In tragicomic anger, she had exploded: "There! Part of my revenge!" The handful of hair she threw at him scattered on the carpet. She declared: "I will not make love with you until they have regrown to their full length. That will teach you, but you are too stupid. Good God, how stupid you can be! And I, too! I love you... No... Yes... You're a turd!"

She locked herself all night long in the bathroom. He banged on the door until dawn. By luck, the neighbors were not home. She didn't relent. She didn't come close to him for seven months. As long as her hair hadn't regained its normal length.

She often scared him. His fear remained linked to the ambrosial blonde tufts of hair strewn on the floor. A spell cast. He had however wanted to see her again. He dreaded this confrontation, though it was necessary for him. After his return to Paris, he couldn't put it off any longer.

Mourad was sitting sideways. He avoided looking her straight in the eyes. He threw furtive glances at her. In the mirror he could observe the whole room. At this time of the day the brasserie was nearly empty. His sullen face lent him a sinister mien. He was unable to put on a casual air. A sort of fog hovered over his physiognomy.

Léa spoke in a soft voice, as if to herself. In a monotonous tone. Silences. Nostalgia of a soliloquy? A hint of lassitude came through. But her facial expression remained hard. A contained violence. She was forcing herself to speak calmly.

He didn't dare confront her. It was she who looked hard at him while screwing up her eyes. Her gaze was strafing, fierce. He felt the shock of the impacts on his lowered brow. Machine-gunned. He hadn't imagined that she could be so brutal. She wasn't. It was he who had pushed her beyond the limit.

Her voice bored through his distressed mind: "I waited for you, you know! I reread all your letters to try and understand. I didn't understand. It was so incomprehensible! You disappeared just like that, without warning, without leaving a trace. Nothing of the sort could have been foreseen.

You had never told me anything. I thought I knew you. To not understand what was happening only increased my despair. Why? I wanted at least a plausible explanation. I kept asking myself and asking myself why did he leave? What did I do wrong? It had to be that. Your escapade was absurd but real! I needed to find some coherence in all that. I had always thought you were agnostic. We had never talked about religion. You made fun of my phobia of priests. You said that religion didn't interest you. I no longer understood. It was all so sudden. So disconcerting. I was crushed."

He couldn't remember what he had written her. They had been short, laconic letters. As if he had feared that he could expose himself in the flow of the writing. Maybe he dreaded the drawbacks of too precise formulations. Maybe he just didn't know what exactly to say. He had to write and that was all! To respect the proprieties. A point of honor. To break up. Three letters, one after the other. To inform her that he was not returning to Paris. That he had enlisted in the struggle of the Afghani mujahideen. Impersonal letters over which time glides without throwing light on their content. The text remains fixed forever. Expressionless. Whenever she would reproach him for his waffling, he would answer invariably: "You know that I can't write. I lack style!" She could reread them ad nauseam without ever being able to cling to a specific expression. "Letters always fall into wrong hands," he had confessed. His mother had systematically burned his father's letters during the revolution… An atavistic terror of being flushed out was a major part of the process. The public writers of the Place d'Armes knew the syndrome very well. They are satisfied by selecting choice morsels from the *Handbook of the Perfect Secretary* that fit the situation. The clients have total confidence in them. Certain writers are specialized in the amphigoric letters necessary for delicate transactions. Their notoriety exceeds the limits of the quarter, even of the town. They are seen as invested with a certain power, but it is never a question of style. Rhetoric is left to the wandering bards and other clowns who, in order to make a living, have to make use of artifice. Their gift of gab is only a trick to con the circle of onlookers. The writers, on the other hand, in the exiguity of their booths, deal with real occasions, not fictions. What they want most is for their procedures to be efficacious. They aim for convincing results. They are professionals who bring important affairs to satisfactory conclusions. An original style deflects the reading from the assigned objective. Such a style is only good for entertainment. Trifles. He too had used the manner of the town writers to compose his correspondence. It was convenient and protected one from literary excesses. Or from being caught out by smugly appropriated words. A neutral, preferably anonymous, formulation will avoid a lot of trouble.

The doleful voice called him back, saying in French: *"Je pleurais comme une madeleine."* Mourad gave a start. He remembered his stupefaction the first time Léa told him how she used to "cry like a madeleine" when she was little. At the beginning he had not dared ask her what this meant. He thought about it for a long time, exploring the meanders of the image. When children dunk their cookie in a bowl of milky coffee or in a cup of tea, there will always be drops dribbling down onto the tablecloth or the apron. Maybe those are the tears of the madeleine… He had finally asked her the question, blushing.

Léa didn't know. This expression seemed obvious to her. She had always used it. She was astonished by this gap in her knowledge. She, who was so fastidious when it came to the exact definition of every word, who was unbeatable when it came to etymologies and synonyms. She always bested him playing Scrabble, doing crosswords or other word puzzles.

Together they looked through the *Larousse*. The explanation had seduced them. For a long time they used the tears of the madeleine as their open sesame.

How many such ready-made French expressions had he learned from her! She gathered them methodically in a little spiral notebook and would comment on them abundantly after dinner for his benefit. Surfacing just then: "rough-and-ready," "the nose to the grindstone."
… Which had helped him a lot in his perception of the French language. It had enriched his locutions and taken the rough edges off his too school-boyish vocabulary. Beautiful images, at times shocking, at times conventional, that were creating an uproar in his soul. A fracas with no echo. A note of spice at the tip of his tongue.

He did not master the French language perfectly, although they spoke it at home. His sister Dalila always brought home the first prize in French. She pulled his leg when she heard him mispronounce certain words or make grammatical mistakes. She would irritate him with a disconcerting phrase: "You didn't suckle the she-wolf!"

Mourad was twenty-four when he got a scholarship for Paris. It was his recompense for being head of his promotion at the USTO. He felt proud and somewhat anxious, but knowing exactly what he would do in the capital of the world and its malefic lights. *City of djinnis and angels,* as the hero of the Egyptian soap opera *Adib* desperately exclaimed. He had watched every episode. The character's candor in relation to his tormented relationship with the prestigious city had intrigued him. He was traveling third class. Paris wasn't like that, he thought. It didn't sound right. A caricature. But he knew from hearsay that the city would swallow up or drive insane anyone who dropped his guard. Before all he was afraid of making himself ridiculous with his Maghribi-inflected French. He spent the summer reading Stendhal and Romain Gary while studying the *Petit Robert* dictionary... Léa had untied his tongue.

She said, articulating slowly: "Yves was there all the time. He did not leave me for a week. He defended you when I would curse you..." That was not surprising. Yves always defended the adversary, especially when the latter was absent, always finding attenuating circumstances. Good old Yves!

He had rendezvous'd at the Epsilon with him, as in the past. Yves hadn't changed. "A real specter, you are! How are you! Sit down." He was happy to see him again. He was beaming. "You look in top shape. Your phone call blew my mind! I am really pleased to see you again." He was squirming like a child in front of the ribbon wrapping a present. Excited and happy to have found his friend again. Gravely: "We were worried for you." Mourad had stiffened. "How typical, he thought. He starts with the indefinite article as usual. He is worse than an Arab!" Mourad knew him well. He knew the detours he would take before coming to the point. Yves was concerned not to upset his interlocutor. "We looked for you everywhere. We got everybody involved. We didn't know what to do. Léa, before all. She didn't understand at all why you bolted. She had a real depression, you know."

Léa!

Love — may God comfort you — starts in laughter and ends in torment... One comes to its truth only by experiencing it. Did the old qadi of Cordoba speak from experience? Had he, as a young man, experienced the gnawing desires of sedition in his flesh? Had the demon appeared to him around about midnight? Unless the deadly desire of the loved One had set him on fire at some dark crossing... The venerable doctor was a crafty old devil like all theologians of his kind. He pontificated knowledgeably on the truth of love for the edification of a few simpletons, and their idly spent youth. He knew nothing of what he advanced and had no need

for it. His ignorance of the tribulations of love gave him the indispensable assurance his office needed. He held forth marvelously on propensity and emotion, and on the art of healing the wound...
Léa!

Mourad had mumbled: "It wasn't easy for me either." He kept on his guard but Yves' babyish, friendly and frank face disarmed him. Yves apologized for bringing back unpleasant memories. "Oh, I have no doubt! I don't judge you, you know. I don't have the right to. You lead your life the way it seems right for you. I may not agree with you but that's neither here nor there. I enjoyed working with you at the lab. You always were full of original and scathing ideas... I've always considered you my friend. Your relationship with Léa concerns only the two of you. There's neither guilty party nor victim. It's life! But you need to know that she nearly died of it. You are well aware of her suicidal character. She stayed cloistered for a full week guzzling vodka without eating. When the ambulance came she weighed just forty kilos! She was completely disoriented by your leaving. Literally annihilated. Sounds caricatural, but it's true!"

Mourad hadn't been able to keep himself from screaming: "I'm a right bastard, that's it? You can't keep yourself from going moral on me, you too?" This bad conscience that was gnawing at him.

Léa murmured tonelessly: "You are a real bastard, you know." Then she shut up as if to give the words the time to do their work. She knew these words would hit him hard. Drill into his flesh. Devastate him. By force of knowing that he was a bastard, he no longer knew what this meant. He anxiously questioned himself. He revived his stock of images. He compared himself ceaselessly to the scumbags he had come across all over and found himself to be different. There was no common measure. He was nothing like those dirty sons of bitches! No way, no comparison possible! And yet, deep down inside, there was something very much like a swamp. It was full of mud. Didn't look pretty at all. It smelled of putrefaction and shit. This ugliness made him feel sick. And yet, did it make him a bastard? There must be a prototype somewhere. The outlines he had in mind didn't help much in identifying the monster. Bad conscience. The voices echoed. Merged. Troubled him. His stomach tightened. Nausea washed over him. Suffocation. He couldn't do anything about it. Anyway, he didn't try to fight it off.

It wasn't the first time Léa called him a bastard. But this time it was no longer just an insulting word. Her heart was heavy with resentment. She unloaded the sorrow that had been weighing her down for a long time now. She wanted to hurt him because of all that pain she had had to deal with by herself. She wanted to make him suffer so that he too would experience the havoc wrought by his departure. She didn't want to take revenge, but wanted him to feel the bitterness overflowing inside her. A lesson, in effect, the objectives of which she hadn't yet defined exactly. Loud and clear. Léa had always been able to hit the bull's-eye when she wanted to. Mourad sensed that he would have to carry a heavier burden. That was it: this accumulation of pain, a sedimentation of accumulated live torments, that she had thrown into his face! Let him deal with it! Vengeance was for later. It was not the order of the day!

Léa had called him a bastard at the very moment he was remembering saying the word to Yves. This coincidence baffled him. A sign? Everything was so stuffed with symbols that in the end they fell apart. A fog on the horizon in which the two disassembled pieces could barely be distinguished. This repressed rage he didn't know about!

Yves was sorry: "Why do you say this? I don't judge you! I haven't criticized you in the least. You are always so absolute in your positions. I don't hold anything against you." He sheepishly wriggled on his chair and then, to ease the atmosphere, asked: "You've been gone more than four years. What did you do all this time, tell me? Say, Mourad, you didn't turn into a fundamentalist, at least? What's happening with the Muslims is terrible. All this blind terrorism!"

Mourad hadn't listened to him. He was chewing over the newly discovered fact that he was a bastard. It didn't help to tell himself that it was just a word thrown about, an inconsequential insult, something was tearing his heart to pieces. Léa was already tormenting him. He had thought he'd left that story far behind, but here he was, taking the plunge again. Diving into a gaping, brackish hole. Unfathomable attraction of the abyss. Breath came with difficulty. He had asked in a flat voice: "Where is Léa now?"

She declared: "I hated you so much!" She paused, then added in a muffled voice: "I still can't stand you." Repeats this a second time. Then, as if hesitating: "I no longer know." The interval of the possible.

...

"She lives in Le Havre. She is married to Pierre, a doctor. Nice guy. She comes to Paris twice a week to attend her courses at Paris-VI. We see each other occasionally. It's no longer the way it used to be. It's terrible! The older you get, the more you work like a slave! Not a moment for yourself. The job eats up all your time. The pressure's unrelenting. You always have to do more. We have researchers who practically never go home! An infernal pace! On top of that, a strong sense of a lack of job security! It's tough! Things are only getting worse in the general grayness." Yves had taken an old notebook from his jacket pocket and leafed through it. "Here's her info. Léa has invited me several times but I haven't managed to go see her yet! Write it down." Mourad had hastily scribbled the phone number on the back of a used metro ticket. "Call her, Mourad. I don't know what her reaction will be, but it's better you do. We could go see her together, if you want?"

Mourad raised his eyes and looked at her. She didn't see him. She was elsewhere, lost in her bitterness. Dwelling on it. What didn't work between them? Good god! The wall. Reinforced concrete!

Mourad had said as if talking to himself: "I have to call her, of course!" He had repeated, solemnly: "Of course." There was a moment of silence.

The waiter had arrived to take their order. "A Coffee!" Yves and Mourad said nothing. They looked at the other customers with an air of absorption. They should be telling each other so much, recount in great detail all that had happened so as to make the time gone by palpable, finding the words needed to journey together beyond the estranging distance. They didn't know how to go about it. They preferred to leave it up to silence to reestablish the fluid ease of friendship. Yves hoped to seal the gap created by Mourad's sudden departure. The latter suffered from not feeling anything as he faced his friend of old. He wasn't there. His mind was wandering along the peaks of Nuristan. Why hadn't he stayed at Abu-l-Qâcim's? The village was a paradise perched high on the mountains...

... The waiter returned with the coffee. He put the check in the middle of the table. Without thinking Yves picked it up and placed it with his own under his saucer. He breathed hard: "All that's past now. Tell what happened! I'm not very well informed when it comes to politics, but I hope that you haven't turned into one of those fanatics like the ones with Ayatollah Khomeyni. Crazy people! But I don't think so. What's up with you? Tell..."

Mourad had lost the habit of telling stories. Those on whose side he had fought didn't speak about themselves. They had been trained in the asceticism of using as few words as possible. They only exchanged conventional greetings, insults or utilitarian idioms with immediate effects. Subtle words were woven only on the loom of intimacy. They were not allowed to spring up unexpectedly. The tongue would turn them over seven times before uttering them. Were those people he had rubbed shoulders with in extreme situations fanatics? What about himself?

How to speak of all this?

She spoke while seeming exterior to her voice: "Yves had sent a fax to your research center. Your boss thought you had returned to Algiers. He too was worried about your silence. I called everywhere. Like a mad woman!"

Mourad looked at him with a feeling of envy, compassion and solitude, then leaned toward him: "Listen, Yves, right now everything is mixed up in my head, but I do need you to do me a favor. It's very important and I do believe that you are the only one who can help me."

Yves was the good Samaritan. A St. Bernard, always there in case he's needed. Present when called. Ready to serve with a wide smile.

…

Her voice trailed off: "Finally Yves convinced me to go and ferret you out in Algeria. Crazy! He came with me to Oran. What an expedition."

…

He had answered without thinking twice. The cry of the heart: "If you need me, I'll be there. Your Allah stories don't interest me! What can I do for you?"

Mourad suddenly grew sad in front of his friend. "That's what it means to be open-handed," he thought. Men of goodwill do exist! He was happy to discover that despite his own ambiguous feelings Yves' friendship remained unshakable. He could ask him without thinking twice. He said in a flat voice: "I plan to move to Australia or New Zealand and I need references to land a job as researcher in a lab. You direct a research team in Sarclay, no?"

Yves eyes opened wide. "Of course! But wouldn't you rather stay here? All's not rosy right now, but maybe we can find a solution. Why do you want to go bury yourself in Australia?" Mourad didn't feel like talking about it. Yves wouldn't understand any way. He only swore by the United States. That's where a major researcher could spread his wings and expect to fully realize his potential. Why bother to leave France if it was to go hide in some hole?! He said, growing slightly animated: "The references are enough! Don't worry about me. I need to get away as far as possible."

After a short silence: "To bury myself, yes, well maybe one has to see things that way; I no longer have a place left on earth!"

He bit his lower lip. What had gotten into him to say such a thing? This shameless tone he had taken! As if he wanted to display wounds so as to be pitied or cajoled. He was not completely in control of himself. Yet Yves didn't seem surprised. He continued to interrogate him feverishly: " What happened to you in Afghanistan, Mourad? You're not some illiterate space cadet, right? Explain, explain yourself!"

...

Mourad had answered in a profoundly depressed voice: "Nothing! Nothing at all! You used to say so yourself, back when, that nothing ever happens to anybody. And you were right. Nothing has happened to me!"

Yves insisted: " I didn't want to be indiscrete, but tell me, did you fight over there? I hear there were horrible massacres! Did you kill people? Why do all that? You were not the kind to have an identity crisis, were you? Or am I wrong? Tell me! You must have lived through extraordinary events that would be fascinating to recount. It isn't everyday that one has a mujahideen at hand. That's a rare species that doesn't hang about the streets of Paris." Yves asked all kind of questions, jumping from one subject to another. He played at being relaxed while being careful not to manifest any negative judgment concerning his friend's choices. He wanted to know only in order to understand him a little better and rekindle their friendship. He had been profoundly perturbed by Mourad's nonsensical behavior. Nothing during the shared years at the university had prepared him for that. They went out together all the time and Yves never questioned their affinities. It was only after Mourad's disappearance that he became aware that there had been a gap between them and that he didn't know what the cause of it was. Their friendship, however, was solid. A true friendship, he would have staked his life on it! Such a friendship couldn't simply vanish like a cloud of butterflies. Even today, in midst and despite of the discomfort of the reunion!

Without answering, Mourad had observed him with a somber mien. He felt something something like vague disapproval. Over there, nobody told anything. To recount engendered inextricable misunderstandings. To tell emptied the soul without consoling it. How to know that the proffered ear isn't blocked?

... He had indeed lived through things that he couldn't recount at present. He was no longer gifted for such an exercise. He had thought about it, however. To do so you would first have to describe the place with a geographer's precision, while stressing the vibration of the trace the place names conceal. And then there is the decor and all of the objects whose description also requires a cosmographer's ingeniousness. But before all there are the men with all the dead they carry... He was incapable of doing it. He saw nothing, or, better his gaze was obsessed by his belly button. By retelling, he would have the impression of justifying himself for no reason. Who was he? This ambiguous question, though he tried to reject it violently, kept coming back to persecute him. Wasn't his identity clearly inscribed on a green card bearing his photo? He was at wits' end. Another one of Léa's phrases! Why did he have to state his identity in order for someone to know who he was? How far did he have to transport his good oar? Was he going to be faced only with judges? He had no faithful dog waiting for him on the shore and that, seeing him from afar, would wag its tail as a sign of recognition, nor did he have a savvy old wet nurse who could recognize him under his disguise.

...

The intonation changed suddenly: "Your mother was very surprised. She thought you were in Paris, with me."

Ah, yes, his mother... "Poor mama!" She had come to get him all the way to Peshawar! He had disappointed her so much! He had relentlessly manhandled her and turned away from her. He had complacently played the role of the ungrateful son. He must have been out of his mind!

The voice went from a joyful skip to a hint of regret: "She's someone, your mother. As you never spoke of her, I didn't imagine her like that at all. In fact I had no sense of her whatsoever. Your mother is amazing. A pity you don't resemble her!"

"That's not so certain," he thought; but he does not want to tell her that. Nor translate for her the proverb that goes through his mind at the same moment: *Kfi l'gedra 'la fummu yashbah ummu.* An Algerian always keeps hanging on to his mother's apron strings. Only the dishes his mother has prepared he will eat until he can eat no more. He can fall asleep peacefully only after she has wished him a good night. It's congenital! Patriarchy is only a trompe l'oeil. He noticed this easily on in his own family. And yet he didn't speak of his mother, but of his father who was very young. He often repeated — Léa pointed it out one day — with a hint of reproach mixed with longing, that his father was very young. His father's youth embarrassed him. When he was in high school he didn't like walking by his father's side because he seemed to be the elder. Many people remarked on this. Mourad didn't know why he was constantly repeating the same thing when he talked about his family. It made him furious.

To think that his mother had undertaken this whole trip just to bring him back home! She had forced his father to come along, for appearances sake. It was she who had done all the footwork. She had a lot of guts. She'd always had guts. During the war of liberation she carried suitcases between Geneva and Chambéry, with Dalila in her arms. She would leave Kamel with a Sicilian neighbor. She would go back and forth twice a week. He had found out in passing that she had lived with his father as husband and wife until Independence. They had gotten married at the Consulate before returning to Oran. A lady! He loved her with a timid love, but he was no longer a child. He stubbornly repressed all reflexes from childhood.

She vents her grievances again: "I was sick after that. I didn't eat. I stayed locked up in my room all day long, curled up under the quilt and the blankets, curtains shut tight. At night I would get stoned in random bars. A true zombie, I was!" He imagined her both prostrate and overexcited by the separation. He remembered her nocturnal wanderings in moments of depression, the morbid rage with which she threw herself into dissolution. All this just to humiliate him. Punish him. For what offense? He hadn't done anything, He had never promised her anything. He had left. It wasn't the end of the world. Why didn't he admit that this could indeed have been the end of her world?

Barely moaning: "I had made holiday plans for the two of us. I was waiting for you. You ruined the lovely summer I had planned on spending with you! I had planned out the smallest detail. Like a little girl dreaming aloud. How stupid of me! I wound up dumped like a stupid bitch!" There had been a question of holidays while he was embarking for Afghanistan! The trip had been chaotic. Tedious formalities, the twists and turns of underdevelopment. A mind boggling circuit. You had to transit through Peshawar. How he had dreamed of that stopover in the midst of the vicissitudes of the journey. The city did not have any of the magic of the *Thousand and One Nights*. He had built a marvelous decor for himself based solely on the name's resonance. What a deception! A small town in shambles! The seedy Orient of documentary films! Faced with the distressing spectacle the entrance into the town offered, he had had the unusual but very real sensation of physically experiencing his own death. He could not express what he had experienced. He had felt neither pain nor exaltation but a kind of nostalgia in a vacuum. A grayish vagueness. He will have to die several times before the final face to face. Dread those trivial successive deaths more than anything.

She raised her voice slightly: "A real bastard, yes! What do you have to say about it all? No need to take that funereal mien! You can spit out whatever you want to, I'm immune. A real bunker! I resisted…"

He didn't answer. He had learned to be wary of her when she took such a slightly detached and disabused tone. She tried to hide her animosity behind a softer inflection of the voice…

She went on: "Yves has told me a little about your oriental delirium. What an asshole! To be so stupid and naïf, it's hopeless. How could I have lived with you for so long without knowing you?! And I, who thought I was bright! I didn't understand a thing. You got to be really gifted!"

He remained silent. It would have surprised him if Yves hadn't given her his report! He was touched by the feeling of helplessness and confusion that suffused her words. He suddenly became aware that she had suffered. And that he had been the artisan of this suffering. That she may never forgive him. A sense of oppression grabbed him by the throat and he distinctly heard his own voice whisper to himself: "You've really made her suffer badly. You can deny it, but it's your fault. You're responsible! She'll hold it against you even if she forgives you. She has no choice." She asked: "So how does the road to Damascus feel? Are you pleased with yourself? Is it exalting? Did you play at being the little soldier or the little apostle?"

Léa's insidious questions freed him from the sense of suffocation. With Afghanistan he was back on mapped territory… It was not a game, alas, or else a very macabre game. An ordeal. A long slack tether the end of which is held by a hardened hand. A thirst. Dismal presentments kept assaulting him. He had become sick with it. During the first ambush, his sphincters had miserably let him down. A rush of disgust and shame had reddened his face, then frozen his body, nailing him to his spot. And yet he had been prepared to face the enemy and to kill or be killed under the most intolerable conditions, without fear or great anguish. It had not lasted long. Long enough, however, to have felt the deep humiliations and absurdity to be covered in his own shit. He would drag that unpleasant feeling with him for quite some time. Like a tinkling that keeps hanging around the tympanum. What had happened afterwards? He couldn't remember any part of it. After the fight he had been applauded. They all had surrounded him and lauded him for having fought like a lion. Although a vile stench emanated from him, no one dared to make the slightest remark concerning his physiological breakdown. The section chief had slipped in a brief allusion to it while slapping him cheerfully on the back: "It's normal, what comes out of the body is Satan's share! That bastard loves to plunge man into the mire! But what matters is the head! That's the only thing that counts. That's where each one of us keeps the fruits of his ventures." The energetic words of his superior had boosted his morale. But this hadn't eradicated the bitter after-taste that filled his mouth whenever he went into combat. Try as he may to repress the slight shiver that was the premise of the degrading symptoms, nothing worked. Fear was knotting his insides, and for a brief instant would block his breath. For a long time now he had managed to control his physical reactions, hiding from this companions — who never ceased to laud his courage and skills — the profound repugnance the crackling of bullets evoked in him. Back in Oran he had read in an English novel that fear was instinctive and courage nothing but this bit of shaky control over oneself that tames this howling beast in the belly. That had made him think. When he had tried to speak about bravery with Hasni, he had noticed with dismay how full of romantic fantasies the latter's mind was. Unlike himself, his friend claimed not to be in the least worried when his patrol was engaged in combat. He said he put himself entirely into the hands of God and that he simply followed the instructions he had been taught to avoid getting wasted. It was absolutely essential to avoid giving in to the insidious pressures of the imagination and the visionary. Otherwise you were done for! "Stop those asshole questions! Can't you see you are terrifying Kadirou? You don't speak of those things. In a fight, instinct rules!", Hasni had screamed one day when Mourad has insisted heavily on wanting to know how his two comrades felt during engagements.

In fact, it didn't interest him that much. Eventually he no longer heeded the slight jolt tightening his stomach. After all, it was just a biological and thus a natural reaction. You couldn't go against nature. He had laughed a lot alone by himself thinking of Buffon and the *Jardin des Plantes*... Nature was an easy mark. He had come to the conclusion that deep down everyone was alone inside his carcass and that whatever was shared with others did not relieve you of yourself. Having meditated for ever on the ephemerality of his existence, he had wound up telling himself: "God — may His name be Glorified — is observing us in silence without worrying about the state we're in." He had quickly corrected himself, scared by the blasphemous character of his thought: "My God, what am I saying? I am blaspheming! Of course He worries and cares about us but that, in turn, does not change the outcome of events. Everyone crosses the bridge from where no one returns alone and with neither clothes nor sandals. A strictly personal and private matter. God is careful not to interfere with our narrownesses."

Hasni and Kadirou agreed that he exaggerated and that if he kept going down this dubious path, God only knew into what dark abyss he risked falling.

... This voice that was turning condescending and hurting him so much. He hated this tone of voice she used when she told him things. Léa berated him openly: "The religious madmen haven't made you more talkative. My poor Mourad, you'll always run away from reality to find refuge in shitty utopias, if it isn't simply by sheer cowardliness. You are incapable of facing up to reality; incapable of facing what troubles you. You always go hide behind your tricks. As soon as things get tough, you run away! You're always making a fuss about everything and for your own benefit alone. Does it give you a hard on to play the hero? Come on, say something! Speak up for yourself!" She invariably sent him back to his pipe dreams.

In front of her he was clumsy and craven. Became obstinate for no good reason. Folded back on himself. Turned a deaf ear.

She was stronger than he. She knew how to face any and all situations while he turned in circles like a snot-nosed brat, only to always and inevitably wind up doing the stupid thing he feared.

He had said with lassitude: "What do you want to know? What do you want me to tell you?"

She looked at him with aversion. Spat at him, ferociously: "You jerk! You really are a creep!"

He mumbled, then his voice grew firmer. "Here you go again. One cannot speak as adults in this situation. What's passed, is passed, Léa. We can't carry those bygones with us eternally. People who leave each other, that's not a rare event in France." He immediately regretted his words. What a boor he was! He couldn't make up for it anymore. He knew from experience that what he had just said was completely absurd. Gratuitously vicious. He didn't believe a word of it himself. Felt bad. This story obsessed him. His brain was going to explode. He didn't understand what had happened either. What was pitching them one against the other. He was exhausted. Why? He loved Léa, but this love hadn't kept him from throwing himself into the abyss. Had he really loved her? What did he know about love? Love, when it is in one's reach and when one can enjoy it in tranquility, isn't love anymore. It's when one loses it for keeps that one discovers its magic! Enough to die insane! Love, one has to repeat it over and over to unveil its arcana. Maybe it is enough to say it, to speak it from the depths of one's heart and guts, again and again, to not be afraid to drivel inanely, in order to see and touch it. He tried to console himself as well as he could, knowing perfectly well, however, that if you miss the light that rises tenderly at night, you can never again see the day. He was groping blindly in the dark. Did he love Léa? Had he loved her? Who to ask? His body had forgotten that which he still kept in memory. Léa knew this better than he did. What a mess!

She had loved him enough to nearly die of it.

Yves had recounted her agony in great detail.

Meanwhile he had been fighting against the communists.

She had loved him to death but she was alive.

The Brotherhood was there! They knew how to exploit the furious anxiety of the self. They formulated good questions. They had all the answers. Life became simple. They hadn't hoodwinked him. His confusion had driven him into their arms. He was looking for certainties in order to escape the questions plaguing him. Afraid of calling himself into question. Of having to search all alone, in fog and cold. Slowly, a sort of melancholia had taken over his gaze. Time was slipping out of his grasp. Food had lost its savor in his mouth. The oriental syndrome! Flight?

"Living, you discover how wretched you are," he thought. Everything he had learned by rote and repetition was miserably foundering on the hackneyed enigma of the sphinx. The number of dead that are the share of everyone's fate. He now reproached himself for having let time slip by without grasping it.

Léa said rudely: "You're not even listening!"

He didn't hear her. He told himself: "One advances, arms and legs numb, what for? The rare moments that present themselves simply disappear in the general brouhaha…" Mourad was listening to himself. He had not been able to answer in good time.

…

Oran, Paris, Birmingham were so far already. He wasn't there anymore.

She said: "You didn't even have the courage to warn me. Thanks for the present! Do you realize how base and despicable your behavior has been?"

He protested softly: "You know that isn't true. I never wanted to hurt you. I don't believe I did."

She spat at him: "You don't believe you did! What do you know of it? You believe you are without reproach?"

He took it on the chin. He didn't want to raise the ante. He didn't like this pathetic scene: an old couple with each one insisting on being in the right against the other, proof in hand. He took a friendly tone: "Listen, let's not tear each other up at this point. None of this concerns us anymore. Tell me what you are doing these days. Yves told me you married a surgeon. How is living in Le Havre?"

She, continuing to speak for herself: "Deep down, you are right. I detest you. I despise you. No. It's only indifference anymore. It's sad, all this love of which not one trace remains. We've never been there! Air! A rag fluttering in the wind! Shadows wandering far from the sun. What triggered all this?"

He said: "No, that's not true. The trace doesn't get effaced just like that. It is simply covered over and then torn by a question that re-emerges. It's difficult to explain. You wouldn't believe me. Anyway, it's incomprehensible for a Western mind."

She shivered, then exploded: "That one takes the cake! A Western mind! Since when do you draw such mentally retarded distinctions? You spent your time pontificating that common sense is the most fairly distributed thing in the world. Have you become totally stupid? Or have you always been that way while I was just blind? Yes, that must be it, given that love is blind! You can strut about!"

He tried to play for time: "That's not what I meant. There is no Orient or Occident, that's all literary crap, but there is a North and a South involved in a struggle to the death. That's real, indeed! It's harsh. Especially if you find yourself on the wrong side. Those who have power have no memory, they have only a few souvenirs and dates which they commemorate with expensive hoopla. The powerless are ravaged by their memory. It's like a curse that sticks to their heels. It hits them hard. It hurts. Religion is like a balm for all that. There is a religious dimension to our make up I had never suspected. Here, one doesn't measure all of its consequences. Its genetic, no joke! It's been going on ever since Saint Augustine! I thought I left because of my disgust with Europe and in search of an authentic identity. Today I no longer know. Afghanistan or Peru, the place doesn't matter. You always carry your own carcass around with you as well as the memory of your own kin. There's no way out... It wasn't easy over there, but I have no regrets. I don't want to go over it again. It's done with, all over. I've learned to see differently, despite all the disappointments... When I left Birmingham I was like one enlightened, devoured by a blazing fire. I was swirling about like a baby bird with barely a feather. I thought I had been reborn. I had wanted that with all my strength. You didn't understand anything I was saying. It's true that I was delirious. But you, the only solution you saw was the psychiatrist! That made me furious. In those days I was dreaming of supernatural powers with which to exterminate all psychiatrists, psychoanalysts and psychologists on earth. I did not need an analyst... I have changed a lot, without getting rid of that abominable other that I ran from. The sincerity of my actions doesn't seem to have had very efficacious results. I've come back exhausted, with empty pockets, and disoriented. I even nearly lost my leg! I have an immense desire for peace. Why does that seem impossible to realize?"

He shut up. How to describe his deserted soul. How to express the desolation and the supplication. The damage to the body, though visible, was much less serious. One endured it somehow! She looked at him in silence. Under the influence of his grotesque confession. He was a shriveled up stranger, that's all! She was surprised to realize how simplistic Mourad's statement had been. She could tell him as much. Explain to him that the colonized had no monopoly on suffering. The rulers also had a memory that haunted them. She knew something about this. Her lips trembled slightly, but she didn't say anything. She examined the commissures of his lips. She suddenly felt exhausted.

He broke the silence in a measured tone: "Today I do not believe in much anymore! It is not because of bitterness, or disappointment or due to some kind of conviction. I haven't learned any kind of detachment. And remain as uncertain and worried as I was in the beginning. I just put up with it, that's all. There's nothing I can do. I needed distance for things to fall back into place."

She said, unable to control her irritation: "For how long are you going to continue running away? Why don't you face yourself? Make a date with yourself and take stock. Make up your mind once and for all. You're in a pitiful state!"

He looked at her and said: "I loved you, Léa. It was inevitable."

She retorted: "I married Pierre to heal from you. Pierre is very good to me!"

Mourad remained perplexed. Were the hostilities breaking out again? It was something completely different. Quickly he took ahold of himself: "You are no longer sick." An intonation that hesitated between question and diagnostic.

Léa didn't answer. She looked fixedly at Mourad for a moment. She looked at the check tickets. She took a purse from her handbag. She paid for the drinks. Mourad watched her ploy without saying anything.

Suddenly she stood up. She said: "Come." She moved towards the exit door. Mourad followed her. She had held her hand out behind her. He took it.

from: *The Master of the Hour*

Lost in thought, Zerrouqi doesn't notice the whitish mass in its halo of fog rising in front of him. Tight, high constructions, like a mass of sugar cubes on the scintillating pan of a pair of scales. The city was gently nodding and crooning in the thickness of noon suspended in a sort of milky scintillation, and seemed to deride him openly. Absurd suggestion of his imagination. Since that morning's paternal reprimand, everything irritates Zerrouqi. He misinterprets the signs he perceives, he is so tired. Enough already. He has been running around the countryside without any rest, his feet are bleeding, you could weep. He was lucky enough to come across a Hillel anchorite who transported him to Blida in the blink of an eye. I'm coming with you, he said, I have a little errand to run. Just by taking him by the hand. He had vanished just as soon as he had deposited him in the ficus alley of the public park. I didn't even thank him. He picked a rose and then slipped away before I could draw a breath. Father Mbarek will clear up this confusion. Now, it all sways a little. A humming sound in the ears. He feels nauseous.

That's Algiers shimmering over there. White as a spread sheet. The city is sticking its tongue out, thumbing its nose at him. It is smirking and showing off its white teeth. Zerrouqi rubs his eyes. I'm not making this up, he says, the city is rustling. Those are not cicadas. It is wrecking his eardrums. He shakes himself, rubs his eyes, bites his arm. Ouch! There can be no doubt, I've made it to Algiers but something's wrong. The city is driving him up the wall. It's unbearable. They'll know who I am. His stick levels a blow at the heap. So there! The mass of the heap sags. It is going to collapse like cardboard scenery. Suddenly the magma rises up again and a booming voice nails Zerrouqi down.

— Hold it, Zerrouqi! Easy, easy, my pretty boy, you're demolishing my town, what's the matter with you? Every lion is master in his own forest. This here is Algiers, little brother, the one you can't force, the Ravishing, the Untamable, the mass and the elite are unstoppable in inventing names to invoke her. The whole world is courting her, the poets pamper her, she is a pearl nestled in her setting. And you, maggot, you dare beat up on her, it's unbelievable. The times are changing indeed... You are far from home, here you are but a tolerated guest, and even then no one so far has invited you to sit down. A bit of savoirvivre and sangfroid! Your manners show a total lack of urbanity. Did your father, may God give him more, forget to teach you good manners by any chance? Hello. Welcome.

— Leave my father where he is, old driveler, Zerrouqi ejaculates, turning crimson. He can't control his irritation and it makes him forget the deference due old age, an impiety. Get out of my way, I have no time to lose with an old fuddy-duddy of your sort, you're bugging me. I have no desire to spend any more time in your jackals' lair, my time is precious. Zoulikha is impatient and I promised her an aubade for tomorrow morning. I'm expected, so out of my way.

— No doubt about it, this is a catastrophe, my poor boy. Have you forgotten the recommendation: when greeted answer with an even more gracious greeting, or at the very least return the greeting. Your father, may God give him strength, has failed in your education for you seem very presumptuous to me, young man. Unless I'm gravely mistaken, there is a strong rural smell about you. You are in Algiers, never forget it, though you seem pretty fickle, Algiers, the Immaculate one with its terraces painted Nile blue, so get rid of your Dahra cow dung and tell me what brought you here, even though there's nothing I don't already know. But God, the merciful one, is more knowledgeable! And concerning your precious time, permit me to shrug it off, you have never even seen a watch, you don't even know what time it is, am I not right? Not knowing it, yet The Hour will come, I nearly hide it so that each soul shall be recompensed according to its works. At this very moment our greatest scientists are pondering the question of how to calculate the hour, but God is more knowledgeable!

He crosses his arms and screws up his eyes to look at him more closely. He offers a large and mocking smile. He's watching him out of the corner of his eye.

Turn your tongue seven times, Mbarek had advised him. This senile old foggy is making me uptight. He must be some big wheel as he held up the city's collapse. Maybe he's the local boss. It's possible that he is only a charlatan, one of those marketplace magicians who trick the credulous natives with their overly ornate sleight of hands, he looks like a bourgeois. One has to be circumspect, master Mbarek kept repeating. I'm in a foreign place, far away from my kin, me, I don't know the customs of the citizens of Algiers. Nobody's informed me or provided me with a travel guide to keep me from falling over my own feet. He bugs the hell out of me, this old ruin, but I gotta be careful, lest I let myself be carried away stupidly. I'm going to change tactics to sound out the mountebank, let me swallow my pride, take a deep breath, there.

— A prayer for the envoy of God! Please permit me to apologize, oh venerable patriarch, this trip has exhausted me, Zerrouqi mutters, with a deferent look. I have lost my bearings and am acting contrary to proprieties.

— Now that is well said, my son, good blood will not lie, you have the brusqueness of your father when he was young, may he forgive this bit of gossip, you'll learn to curb it as you grow older. God loves those who persevere! That wasn't too difficult, was it, now let's see what brought you here? Open your heart to me.

Turn your tongue seven times. He is provoking me, pushing me to talk about dad, maybe he wants to unsettle me, but I won't say a word. He seems to have known him well and he knows my name and pedigree. There must be an explanation. I'm not going to let myself be taken by surprise, honey it up, the old ones, they like it sweet and sugary.

— Honorable hadj, I am here on family business.

— Oh, what amazing progress your language is making. You are alert. By the Tabernacle of Lights, what a metamorphosis. I'm tickled. You are a good offspring, you have potential, most certainly, you will be the equal of your father, the well-named.

Zerrouqi has a tough time controlling a trembling in his cheekbones. You can shove my father up your butt. He keeps clenching and unclenching his jaw. Relax, smile, that tottery old ruin is putting me on. Maybe he believes he is putting me at ease. There are people who, behind a delightful folksy attitude have the knack to make you furious.

— Tell me, noble hadj, with whom do I have the honor of conversing? I have neglected to ask you for your name, although such a question should be asked only once salt and water have been shared.

— Okay, son, I'll drop it, the caustic wit and the irony. I am Sidi Abderrahmân, the patron saint of Algiers. Normally I travel on a flying carpet but I only have one. Yesterday, at the Madrague, our port, the gulls sullied it a bit and my good Mimouna is in the process of cleaning it. Today is her washing day. I saw you come from afar, I couldn't drop my beloved city, that lions' den, even if you have good reasons to be angered by it. What would the good people say? After all I am the protector of these places, as it is good to remind the newcomers from time to time. What would be our purpose otherwise? They nickname her "The Warrior." Such descriptions abound, I gather them in my diary, oh, just a little notebook, for the fun of it. The writing of a journal presupposes a relationship to being as particular, something our climate does not predispose us to. I quite like this one, listen: Seen from the high seas, Algiers resembles in form and color a parrot sail spread over a green field; the mountains that surround it, a well-cultivated countryside all covered with white houses among which there are at times magnificent buildings, present, as you draw closer, one of the most beautiful vistas offered by the Mediterranean coastline. Great works have been undertaken to fortify all the seaside points that permit approach, and, despite all that, Algiers offers nearly no defense when approached from the land. You had the proof of that just now. Come with me, we'll go to Serkadji to fetch Habshi's, your brother's, head, don't ask me how come I know all this. Time is short and space narrow, only God is omniscient!

Zerrouqi's eyes open wide. There is no power but… Father Mbarek says so often, this world is but illusion. Didn't Sidi Abderrahmân die two centuries ago? Could there be a second one? In which case he couldn't be the city's patron saint. He keeps silent for fear of appearing oafish. He follows on the heels of the venerable saint all the while exhaling the name of the Highest One, to put up a good show. Mbarek will shed light on all this after he returns. Father Mbarek, I won't leave you for a minute, you'll give me all the answers. Meanwhile, he rejoices, puffs himself up, he'd roll around on the ground if the other wasn't there. There'd be reason for it, as Algiers is listing lamentably. She's twisted, crooked, leaning this way and that, and will remain so forever. The miracle-worker, patron saint though he may be, did not pull it back up correctly. The doddery old man will bite his nails for it. In the bone, me lord, he gave it a good whooping.

This will certainly be remembered beyond the seventh generation.

ESSAYS

MAGHRIBI SURREALISM

SURREALISM IN THE MAGHRIB
SURREALIST MAGHRIB
THE MAGHRIBIAN SURREALISTS
MAGHRIBIAN SURREALITY
THE SURREALIST REVOLUTION IN THE MAGHRIB
SURREALIST MAGHRIB PRESS SERVICE
SURREALISM IN THE SERVICE OF THE MAGHRIB
Etc.

— Given an audience of intelligent participants
— Into a red chechia without a ponytail place nine ping-pong balls
numbered from 1 to 9.
— Shake the chechia for the one minute needed to create silence.
— Draw a ball
— The number on it determines the title of the essay.
...except that, well, the balls have disappeared.
Which proves that a chechia is as good as a top hat.

The Maghribian, *"that inveterate dreamer, daily more discontent with his destiny, has trouble assessing the objects he has been led to use"* (objects are not very numerous, one has to add, because a subtle lack surrounds his gaze and turns him away from *"real life"*), *"objects that his nonchalance has brought his way, or that he has earned through his own efforts, almost always through his own efforts, for he has agreed to work, at least he has not refused to try his luck (or what he calls his luck!)."* This luck is not a Straight Way: it is uncertainty — like the piece of clothing one no longer takes the pains to mend. However, he values this luck he has awaited at the end of a cold weapon, he hopes for at a border crossing. For its sake, he has accepted all kinds of exile. *"At this point he feels extremely modest,"* but nobody should be fooled: it is a loaded silence!

Who is this Maghribian? How to define him?

"The woods are white or black" despite the gone-to-earth nuances. Today definition impassions because of its implications. A domain for going astray. Political jealousy far away from the exploded sense of the true.

Indeed there does exist a divided space called the Maghrib but the Maghribian is always elsewhere. And that is where he fulfills himself.

Jugurtha lacked money to buy Rome.

Tariq gave his name to a Spanish mountain.

Ibn Khaldun found himself obliged to hand over his steed to Tamerlane.

Abd el Krim corresponded with the Third International.

...

An excessive taste for history and controversy chains him ironically to a hastily exploited hagiography. As to the Tragic, he only grasps its throbbing and banal spark. He turns his back on the sea and mistrusts the sun, knowing its terrible burns. *"The mere word freedom is the only one that still excites him. (...) It doubtlessly satisfies [his] only legitimate aspiration."*

"There remains madness." Around here it is common. It circulates. Sometimes it gets locked up, by accident. For the rest of the time one prefers to tame it in order to enjoy it in the margins of the NORM. Because from very early on everyone learns how best to exploit it. Knowing that *"hallucinations, illusions, etcetera, are not a source of trifling pleasure."*...

I council the reasonable man to go sit by the river and he will see pass by all the madmen he ever wanted to meet; provided that he live long enough.

All Maghribians know the subversive power of madness; their artists (with rare exceptions) know it less well than they do, as shown by the sugary and lukewarm use they make of it in their works trying to compel the unbearable limits of a dailyness so difficult to bear.

The madman, the mahbûl, the medjnûn, the dervish, the makhbût, the msaqqaf, the mtaktak, etcetera, belongs to folklore, alas. This reduction reveals the narrowness of the outlook.

It happens, however, that the jerky flood of fire and mud illuminates the word: *Nedjma* bears witness to this just as some of Khaïr-Eddine's bursts carry its disorder.

On the screen, madness remains a moving picture. Maghribian movie makers — the Algerians in particular — are seduced by the image of the madman: he is thought to speak what had been silenced. In most cases we are dealing with postcard-madmen (colonial exoticism was fond of this sort of postcards), boring and pompous. Zinet's in *Tahia ya Didou* does grab me, maybe because of its naïve clumsiness.

...

Of the dream and the marvelous, the Maghribian knows the weight: it is a nod of the head and a long sigh.

In the morning the one who has dreamed tells someone close: I had a dream. Then shuts up. The other one has to answer: oh well, by the grace of God. Only then does he tell his dream.

I have let many dreams pass by for not having been able to say the hallowed formula in time.

I have also known many Maghribians said to be married to Djinnies or Rûhanies — floaty creatures between the human and the angelic. According to their entourage things weren't any worse than for other couples: quarrels and reconciliations, broken dishes and careful housekeeping.

In the Maghrib the ancestors often visit the living for the sheer pleasure of appearances.

For a long time the Maghribian has been a surrealist without knowing it. Take for example the following statement by Ibn Arabi:

"In what I have written I have never had a deliberate purpose, like other writers. Glimmers of divine inspiration illuminated and nearly overcame me, so that I couldn't free my mind of them except by writing down what they revealed to me. If my works show any kind of formal composition, this form is not intentional. I have written some of my works on the behest of Allah, sent to me during my sleep or through a revelation."

But Breton has defined surrealism *"once and for all"*: *"SURREALISM, n. Psychic automatism in its pure state, by which one proposes to express — verbally, by means of the written word, or in any other manner — the actual functioning of thought. Dictated by thought, in the absence of any control exercised by reason, exempt from any aesthetic or moral concern." "ENCYCLOPEDIA. Philosophy. Surrealism is based on the belief in the superior reality of certain forms of previously neglected associations, in the omnipotence of the dream, in the disinterested play of thought. It tends to ruin once and for all other psychic mechanisms and to substitute itself for them in solving all the principal problems of life. (…)"*

During the twenties, some Maghribians in exile *"performed acts of Relative SURREALISM."* It was difficult for them to do otherwise: the family was a lack they wept over in front of a post office window, the fatherland a confiscated identity and religion a recognition.

Today the twenties are long gone, drowned in the gaze. The *"fish"* have dissolved and fat rats are enthroned as critics. *"The Magnetic Fields"* lie fallow. Only the battlefields are exploited.

The *"act of ABSOLUTE SURREALISM"* remains to be done.

Premonitory signs announce it.

"...
....
....
....
...."

"Etcetera."

The passing Maghribian is surrealist in Djeha.
Nafzawi is surrealist in sexual revelation.
Ibn Khaldûn is surrealist in intrigue.
Sidi Ahmed ben Yussef is surrealist in cursing.
Mejdûb is surrealist in anguish.
Feraûn is surrealist in Si Mohand.
Kateb is surrealist in the tradition.
Dib is surrealist in the drift.
Mrabet is surrealist in his joints.
Sénac is surrealist in the streets.
Khaïr-Eddine is surrealist in his alcoholic delirium.
I am surrealist when I am not there.
Tibouchi is surrealist in certain verses.
Baya is not surrealist despite Breton's sympathy.
Etcetera.

"I would like to stress this point: they are not always Surrealists (…) because they did not want to serve simply to orchestrate the marvelous score."

This *"marvelous score"* we find it in the game of the boqala, in the threnody of the professional mourner, in the rhymed recitation of the meddah, in the invocations of amorous magic, in blasphemous insults, etcetera. Speech and gesture are not dissociated from the perpetual movement of the natural elements that encumber the waking dream. Superb and indifferent echo, assonances. The lines are established, bent to the severity of chance: there is nothing to prove.

The Maghribian artists, however, are often obsessed by their image, they want to prove something: that they have *"talent."*

A left bank Parisian publisher confided confidentially that he did not like to do business with Maghribian writers because they all think they are Rimbaud.

So what!

It is certain that he, Rimbaud, didn't give a damn about being a Maghribian in the Harrar and that the publisher in question is a cad despite his undeniable qualities.

Today this obsession with *"talent"* keeps most Maghribian artists from being *"modest recording instruments."* Kateb is to my knowledge the only one who denies *"the 'talent' which has been lent to [him],"* but he has lost his resonance. His suicidal position enchants only the drifters closing in on him. I would have loved to hear him exclaim: *"The haste some show to see me disappear and the natural taste I have for agitation alone would be enough to dissuade me from vainly shuffling off this coil"*...

The Maghribian artists have plenty of *"talent"* — but not enough to dare say *"We have no talent, (...)."*

One had to be rotten through and through with culture and have a moral rigor above suspicion in order to lance the boil. "(Even) *the simplest surrealist act"* demands a considerable subconscious disposition. One does not go *"into the street"* on a whim and, in order to make art fade away one has to be a familiar of its arcana.

We will certainly manage to melt ourselves into the surreality of our space in order, finally, to be.

Right now the *"recording instruments"* are somewhat gummed up.

"There still exists at this hour throughout the world (Isn't the Maghrib the beginning and the end of the world? It is said that Atlas is wearying under his load. It is also said that the world is a miniature Maghrib but

that everyone does their best to ignore this fact), *in the high schools, in the workshops, in the streets, in the seminaries and in the barracks young, pure beings who refuse to fit in."*

One of those *"young beings"* went to Tunis high school. To a French Literature exam question on *"qu'est-ce qu'un beau vers?"* (what is a beautiful verse?) he answered: *"un beau vers est un ver à soie"* (a beautiful verse is a silk worm)*. But since then he has had the unhappy naïveté to take himself for an inspired poet!… This often happens and is, when all is said and done, less problematic than the case of the "pen pimps" who set themselves up as censors of taste. That's because many *"corpse(s)"* don't give up the hope of *"making dust."* I'll leave them to their sordid haggling, necrophilia not being one of my pleasures.

It is finally into Maghribian Sufism that surrealist subversion inserts itself: *"Psychic automatism in its pure state," "amour fou,"* revolt, chance meetings, etcetera.

The mistrust Sufism inspires and the multiple attempts at recuperating it incite me to be more attentive towards a phenomenon it is wrong to hastily catalogue as retrograde. A judgment based on ignorance!

There always exists a non(?)-conscious smidgen of Sufism in the Maghribian writer who is not a clever faker — just reread Kateb or Khaïr-Eddine, for example.

The Maghribian rarely errs concerning the derailment of his Sufis: in this domain, mystification is not easy. Where the exterior observer sees only heresy, sexual dissoluteness, coarse language, incoherent acts, etcetera, he asks himself:
— Yes?
— Yes!… No.
It's obvious, *"Existence is elsewhere."*
Thus goes *"belief in life (…)"*…
When the Sufi Master is not present, the initiates don't dance.
You will have understood, or at least I hope so, that despite my perverse attachment to art, it is *"elsewhere"* that I hope to sojourn.
The Surrealist Revolution is total and *"in matters of revolt none of us can have need of ancestors."*

Constantine — March 7, 1981.

---

* Tengour's pun on the homophony of vers = verse and ver = worm is untranslatable.

UNDESIRABLE WITNESS

1. The poet is responsible to poetry, that is to say no "superior injunction" may be invoked to justify failure in this regard. *"The implacable redness of Cain"* cannot sober up the muse from her sacred drunkenness.
...

But to know this and to adhere to it while sharing Goethe's formula, "to demand intentions and goals from the artist means ruining his trade," cannot make me hide from view the murderous triviality of my country's dailyness. For despite "inhabiting poetry," I move about with a national identity that anchors me in a political space. I don't want to, nor can I, get rid of it despite the many troubles it causes me. I am Algerian. A fact that's not at all extraordinary. After all, Baudelaire was French!

"All those who fall" today in Algeria — much despite themselves for many — in a way bear witness to this circumstantial link with the group of origin. The tribe, jealous of its prerogatives, worries about the least outbursts from one of its own. "I" is a "We" that must not think "Other." It is up to him who experiments with walking on "untrodden paths" to run all the risks; and he who imagined himself free as the wind — this child "with hands full of innocence" — suddenly he is called to account. The tribunal, before which his case is brought, distrusts the "penman's hand" that does not follow its dictation, as much as the "ploughman's hand" when it ploughs beyond its fields. All these hands are to be cut off in a century in which light is waning even as electricity has yet to extend across the whole of the planet.

*

2. We are not without knowing the double anathema that strikes the poet: undesirable trouble-maker in Plato's *polis,* see how he goes astray in the vanity and delusion of his talk, God not having recognized him as his spokesman. Thus the Prophet joins the philosopher in condemning a fictional poetic utterance as illusory and vain. The pretension of poetry — "interior image which hearing fingers" — to be a pathway to knowledge, to know how to discover the world and find truth, in short, to produce fundamental sense amidst the perpetual din of ideas, can only lead

to unreason, the impasse taken by the bad angel imbued with his own brilliance. However, as Kateb Yacine remarked so justly: *"Mohammed had all the trouble in the world trying to impose his koranic tutelage on the Arab poets... but these quarrels touch us little, poetry can never be banned."* That's why they are dead set on killing the poets or excluding them from the community.

And yet I wonder about my dead friends: Wasn't Tahar Djaout assassinated because his anti-fundamentalist journalistic writings disturbed by hitting the mark? Wasn't Youcef Sebti assassinated because of his "consciousness raising" activity among the students of the El Harrach National Institute of Agronomy? Wasn't Abdelkader Alloula assassinated because he was a communist? And wasn't Bakhti Benouada assassinated because he worked at being a link between "Arabophone" and "Francophone" intellectuals and artists? And the others...? All, despite the differences of their aesthetic projects, were partisans of a resolutely anti-Islamic "social contract" and had made their stance public. It was their "political" struggle for a modern society many tried to eradicate that made them targets. Literature and art hold such a minor place in the vision of the "Islamic" world and of Algerians in general, that only the artist's social activism and the most obvious levels of his art — i.e. its political, ideological and normative implications; the external, modifiable aspect — are censored.

*

3. At bottom, what the group commands the poet to do, is to raise it up high in his chant. He is its herald. Poetry has no other function than to comfort and exalt the group's nerve, its "'açabiyya," favoring the turbulence of the bond. This done, the poet can go play his favorite games in order to produce a sublime and shine in his gorgeous finery. The group becomes more demanding and "nervous" as its cohesion diminishes and its preeminence over individuals vanishes. It accepts the hooligan (ça'lûk) because he is the extreme incarnation of the tribal norms. His solitude is a consequence of his excesses. Shanfara can proclaim: I have widowed women, orphaned children, I came back the same as I was when I left and night is even blacker. He is forced to take refuge in inaccessible places. His marginality and (poetic) license exalt the group in which they find a place that is not negligible. But the barely emerging individual demands that one

wring the neck of eloquence in order to be *absolutely modern*. Such a one inscribes himself in the break and into errancy. Si Mohand U'Mhand preferred the tavern to the august assembly. It is true that colonization had accelerated the process of disintegration.

*

4. I notice that most Maghribi artists are elsewhere, without, for all that, having penetrated *"the true life."* They haven't sought out that life. True or false, that means disappointments all around. The soil still sticks to the shoes. Could the Maghrib (and Algeria in particular) be carried by those who have left it or aim to do so? In which case the poet's errancy, his voluntary or forced exile, his expatriation would bear witness to the profound reality of his group of origin. By leaving the "circle of reprisals," he relegates his kin to the margins of the world. His voice would be other/highly critical if it also took its distance from the hotchpotch of this world.

Genoa, 15 February 1996

ON RAÏ

For a long time, raï was considered an obscenity. One couldn't decently listen to it in a family setting, unlike Andalusian, *cha'bî* or Saharan music. Around the *meïda* (the low table that gave the indispensable exotic touch to indigenist literature), the Algerian family tastes the pleasures of the belly without refusing those of the mind and heart. Postcards guarantee it. Shame *(hashma),* the cardinal virtue of the lineage, forbade a music judged to be depraved access to *good bourgeois homes.* In those days, in the poor quarters of the city, it had to be mentioned at the entrance, on a wooden tablet hung from the lintel, in order to avoid any possible confusion that could have bloody consequences — for death was rarely idle. The razors' searing intensity. The blood boiling over in the gutter as in Lorca.

Of its origins — ripe with controversy! — raï has kept the acrid harshness and murky glitter of the dives and brothels of Oran, Relizane and Bel Abbès. For the good city dweller of Tlemcen or Mostaganem, a certain bad taste — that of the bad boys and lost girls, of the rootless invaders of cities — transpires in every note, every intonation, **every** movement. All he can see in raï is the uncouthness of shoeless goatherds, the base exaltation of vileness, the triumph of instinct over soul. Which explains its repression.

In my early childhood I heard all tones indiscriminately. The Moorish cafés of Tigditt, those of the lower suika or of Qadous el Meddah, broadcast the songs without worrying about the scratchy phonographs. The exclusivity of membership and the jealous care lavished on distinction ensured that one did not mix the genres; thus each place proudly confined itself to a music imposed by the taste of its clients. No matter the genre, the highest quality was required. There were constant arguments about some minor detail of the melody or about an inappropriate word. The specialists pulled a face.

The struggle for independence has hatched other sounds in the fracas of revolution. Before all it has imposed the silence of the augural expectation.

Today, as another silence grips the Algerian landscape, I begin to see the painful and tragic consequences of the measures of austerity taken in those early days. (Certain perverse exegetes, due to impaired hearing no doubt, have always considered music to be the devil's invention...)

Native grade school and then high school taught me to appreciate other sonorities by slowly draining the inherited ones towards folklore. My late meeting with raï was due to chance. Perhaps I can speak to it, but to transcribe it seems pointless. Oran had never looked as beautiful to me than during that spring of 1987! Captive, I jubilated. The various elements came together in a sudden bedazzlement. I was immersed in raï, a passionate drama, similar to what had happened with the blues during my adolescence, except that the intonations of raï scoured the depth of my memory. I enjoyed the moment deeply with the troubled sense of reliving it half in joy, half in pain. Banality of the great moments of tension. Interior distortions! *Wahran, Wahran, ruhtî khsâra (Oran, Oran, what a waste!)*

The mediatisation of raï since the '80s, first in Algeria, then in France and throughout the world, corresponds to a social phenomenon. Which doesn't explain much. This kind of phenomenon rightfully scorns any explanation. "The facts are hard-headed," Lenin used to say, but what does the hard-headedness of a music mean at the moment of a debacle?! The fear of a savage flood from the working-class suburbs may not be foreign to the interest invested in raï, rap and other marginal forms of expression. Rumblings of anger. But the essence of raï is elsewhere!

"Ana bhar 'aliya wa ntiya llâ" (I'm screwed, but you're not...)
This leitmotiv of the raï song — it arises unexpectedly from each text like a collective signature — translates the cry of love and existential revolt of an Algerian youth that is lost, idle and out of work in an quickly disintegrating urban space. It is from this crumbling younger generation, trying to grab life with both hands without worrying about any other form of identity quest, that raï draws its power and brilliance. A youth that no longer revels in big words, eyes and ears wide open. *Idle*, by malediction. It does not want to lose itself without having spent all of its resources.

Indeed, raï is the music of the young ones, the *chebs*. They are numerous in Algeria: cheb Hasni (assassinated in Oran in February 1995), cheba Fadila, cheb Khaled, cheb Mami, cheb Sahraoui, cheba Zahouania, etc. Many leave the country, not understanding why they, who dwell at the core of their public's (the people's?) frustrations, have become targets. Exile is their trade.

When questioned, raï singers deny being politically motivated. They say all they sing is sharp desire and *amour fou*, the definitive crossing and the daily problems of the young. "Problem" is a recurring word of Algerian parlance which they pick up on ad nauseam. They recite the Shahada in their concerts and naively confess to not understanding anything about the ploys of politics. Far from being stupid, they are aware that singing has become illicit. They go on singing because they enjoy it, because their public demands it and because, deep down, death is nothing.

Once upon a time, during the colonial era, the masters *(sheikh* and *sheikha)* of Oranian song, such as sheikh Khaldi, sheikh Hamada, sheikha Rémiti were the keepers of traditional Beduin culture whose mode of artistic expression was the poetry called *melhoun*. They had a double repertory:

— The audible, built on didactic and religious matters, questions of love and praise, and on the perpetuation of the group's unadulterated values. This register was that of the votive feasts of the tribe's saints, of marriages, circumcisions, etc. It was the site of living memory and of the underground resistance to colonial occupation. Here the masters communicated with their audience in shared aesthetic representations. Values remained solid.

— The unsayable, the forbidden, the repressed, what is unleashed when language bursts forth raw, brutal and proud of its transgressions. This register was reserved for small, limited audiences and for the places of bad renown. There the innovations were numerous and often illegal in the eyes of the censors. There lie the roots of raï, which will develop in the seventies as traditional Algerian society starts to disintegrate.

"Where does the name 'raï' come from?" I had asked the taxi driver on the road from Oran to Mostaganem. The car's radio-cassette player was blaring. "It makes you lose your head!" he had answered automatically. *Châb al bâroud* crackled on the player. It didn't bother the driver. He upped the volume and shook his head as a connoisseur would. Today's version, sung by cheb Khaled has nothing to do any longer with the nationalist epic of the thirties, which conjures up the "baroudeurs," the fighters that were the companions of the Emir Abdelkader.

Raï is the desire-scream of that which can never be: the searing intensity of the moment that leaves no trace one could contemplate later on in a nostalgic unveiling of the soul. It is an open wound that never scarifies. In it the most diverse references come together: a crossbreeding at times successful, often hybrid, but always bearing witness to the disjunctions of an

Algerian youth starved for life. Here love walks on the wild side. The brutality of desire lights up the flesh without any other intention than the imperfect jouissance of the occasion (as an example, the famous provocative refrain sung as a duo by Hasni and Zahouania: *Derna l'amour fi barraka mranaka / We have made love in a shaky shed*).

But the lack of manners and of courtesy in no way prevents the total gift of self by the one — boy or girl — who is gripped by love. An unexpected love, defying all efficient planning. How not to be enthralled by the beauty of this plaint: *Galbi bgha l'bayda wa zerga 'lâh djât/ My heart desired the white, why did the blue (black, brown) come?* indicating the struck lover's surprise at the sudden apparition of the unexpected loved one. This simple question unfolds the surprising pain where bad luck pitilessly hammers the disoriented young man.

The violence of the scream breaks all chains, all barriers; it scares the thirsty bird above the head. Raï stands solidly on the ground where one has to dance.

But already blood and exile call us to other dérives...

From: *The Master of the Hour*

On the marketplace in Tigditt there were skillful storytellers. They had mastered the art of holding an audience spellbound while recounting the wonders of the saints of the Dahra. Hagiography is one of the most beloved forms of popular narratives in the Maghrib, and especially in Mostaganem where I grew up under the benevolent protection of the saints. It consists of an often fragmentary narrative where the situation wins out over the psychology of the characters and the local atmosphere renders description unnecessary. Our tale tellers knew how to take advantage of the fragmentation of the story. They would insert whatever digressions they felt would make the exchange more lively. Their witticisms were welcomed with gales of laughter and applause. We — the Suika gang — listened to them avidly. We were credulous, wonders enchanted us. The verve of the storyteller would transport us into a world that was as marvelous as that of the movies in the Ciné Lux or the Alhambra. I trembled with pleasure, certain that those fabulous creatures were going around incognito and that one of them could address me suddenly on the corner of 21st or 33rd street to ask for directions or a specific address. You had to be vigilant not to miss the occasion that would allow you to fulfill your destiny by uncovering the true identity of the stranger and knowing how to respond. We would talk about this in our evening discussions, sitting on the sidewalk. We would elaborate tortuous plans meant to guard against all eventualities.

In those days assassinations and house searches were common in the quarter. People would "go away." Those who were arrested were tortured. Rural refugees swelled the shanty towns. In the houses, those who had radios secretly listened to *The Voice of the Arabs*... There were new words like "organization," "revolution," "congress"... We all wanted to grow up to "go to the mountains." We were impatient, but none of that kept me from being attentive to the *Thousand and One Nights,* to the epic tale of Antar bnu Chaddâd or of Malik Seyf and the turbulent Dhara marabouts. My grandfather knew how to tell a story. Every night I made him tell me a story so that nightmares would not disturb my sleep.

I would also go listen to the public storytellers in Qadûs al-Meddah. There was a fountain there and it was said that a long time ago there was a storyteller who captivated all the men of the town so that even the muezzin would forget the call to prayer. Was the place named so as to warn the faithful against the dangers of fiction or wasn't it rather to seal the jubilation of listening into memory?

All stories are not equivalent. In hagiography, the hero of the story is a saint — man or woman — whose wonders are recounted so as to edify the audience. The narrator doesn't try to entertain his public but, by focusing its attention on the proposed metaphors, wants to make it conscious of the vanity of the world and the perpetuity of the Creator. All fiction is banned from the tale. The story is not a simple phantasmic "saying," product of some poetic aberration, but a "doing" in the sense that it operates a change during the listening. The oral tradition proudly believes in the efficacy of its words.

There was also the Jeanmaire public school, where Mr. Martin taught us the fables of La Fontaine and the adventures of Tartarin of Tarascon. On Wednesdays, he would make us read *Tarzan* in a large-sized illustrated book with a hard cover.

This childhood keeps today's adult in the precarious equilibrium of a poetic trajectory. To return to the "dark centuries" in order to come face to face with a certain concept of *Bildung* has a purpose: to scrutinize collective memory and take pleasure in following its convolutions while carefully avoiding falling into any of the holes strewn along its course. This enterprise is not new, I believe there has always been someone who stood up in the marketplace without fearing the crowd's vindictiveness. Today I hear the vociferations of the so-called nationalists and I don't understand. I don't understand my perplexity. Where is the light of my childhood? That of the sura which Sheikh 'Adda had us repeat endlessly… The horizon of the eighties has only brought forth frustrations and self-hatred. Independence has become a trivialized word emptied of its emotional charge. The colors of the flag regain their brightness only in the clamor of over-exited soccer stadiums.

… The urgency, who could doubt it, is relative. The Algerian writer is not condemned to bear witness to a bloody course of events, but has to speak freely. This freedom, which some want to deny him, is precious, as it is the open sesame of unsuspected treasures and pains. It is, at any rate, the guarantor of writing. Nobody is asking anything of us and yet we have to act as if the injunction was there. It is there, assuredly. We have to find the words and the form to say the chaos, at least the part of it we can perceive, without boasting. The stakes are high.

Why a hagiography, when religious zealots everywhere arrogantly manipulate the sacred? Maybe exactly because of this. It is not a question of playing at riddles, all is said in the text.

At least I hope so.

Villa Waldberta, Friday, 25 May 2007

"THE BELLY IS STILL FECUND"

From the Villa Waldberta, it seems far away. But I am Algerian and what happens over there touches me. To speak out is necessary to contain the emotion and try to understand what remains incomprehensible to me and many others like me. Despite the fact that I have written *The Old Man of the Mountain* and *Moses' Fish*, the violence of facts always remains surprising and dismaying. Distance does not diminish the shock, it demands that it be examined attentively if one doesn't want to cut oneself off from the country. Listening to the news on Canal-Algerie, to the debates, to the people interviewed or to those who call the station, and by following the preparations for the demonstrations "against violence — for national reconciliation" in all the wilayas, I am profoundly saddened by the masquerade of the staging. "This is not how one waters the camels, o Saad!" we are warned by the first proverb of the Arab tradition. It is not by hammering home the benefits of civil harmony and the foresight of the President of the Republic or claiming "That's not true Islam!" that one exorcises the beast. Algeria has been engaged in civil war since 1986 and what has happened these last days, despite its spectacular nature, is but a tragic episode of that crisis. "Facts are hard-headed," and we have to look at them rather than occult them or "stupidly stare" at them.

Why say that everything's all right and that the Algerians are reconciled between and with themselves when living from day to day only creates worries, anguish and disgust with life? For the young ones, especially, when one pays attention to what they are saying, daily life is abysmal. Their songs only speak of ways of escaping from that hell. How then not to wish for the paradise promised to the martyrs?

"The suicide attack is not part of our sunni traditions," some will cry out in outrage, but the Maghrib has not always been sunnite and the traditions know how to adapt to the rhythms of the times.

Police and military actions — the Algerian state, after a few hesitations, has known how to make use of these perfectly — can momentarily contain terrorism but do not suppress the causes that permit it to be reborn from its ashes. How to eradicate these causes, and, first, what are these causes, "that's the question"?!

I won't pretend to possess the keys of the problem but will only, like the child in the tale watching the royal carriage pass by, say my surprise that nobody sees that the king's naked.

Algeria is rich, we are told, the state coffers are full, the trade balance is positive, etcetera. The armed groups no longer terrorize the countryside, nor do they rule over the popular quarters in the cities, etcetera. It is totally safe to move about, wherever and at whatever hour of the day or night, etcetera. And yet no dynamic seems able to propel the country towards that state of improvement the sycophants keep proclaiming.

But let's move on, for what has just happened in Algiers may concern a different history/story, the one of which al-Qaïda dreams, namely the place of "Islam" in globalization. Whatever the manipulations that presided over the birth of Islamic fundamentalism, the fact remains that it is nourished and strengthened by the oppression and injustice of a world order dominated by the United States. Muslims, and more specifically the Arabs, have yet to come to terms with their past greatness. Many attribute their decadence to the relinquishment of the values of Islam. Those are only phantasms, but the imaginary carries considerable weight in the affirmation of identity. That coming to terms is made all the more difficult due to Israel's refusal to consider the rights of the Palestinians whom their army cheerfully smashes, to the military occupation of Iraq, to the way the Arab regimes oppress their people, etcetera. In such a context, the bloody utopia propagated by al-Qaïda is a balm. That it is totally chimerical does not matter to the young man who goes to blow himself up in a public space in Algiers or in London, Jerusalem or Madrid… Theological arguments or police and military pursuit of "terrorism" does not resolve the question of the world order. There's a foul smell in here!

Seen from that angle, Algeria is a reservoir of martyrs.

"Now is the time of the assassins…" (Rimbaud)

IN THE VALLEY OF THE UNFINISHED

1. First of all, a reminder:

wa ash-shu'arâ'u yatba'uhumu al-ghâwûna / 'Alam tara 'annahumu fî kulli wâdin yahîmûna / wa 'annahum yaqûlûna mâ lâ yaf'alûna... (And the Poets, — It is those straying in Evil, who follow them: Seest thou not that they wander distracted in every valley? — And that they say what they practice not?) (Qur'an, Sura XXVI, 224-226, translation Yusuf Ali)

How does this divine word work on us, US: an *umma* by force of circumstance? (as things get diluted there remains but force or rather oppression). Of what order is the anathema on poetry? (or disorder?) Is it a matter of a simple warning linked to a particular circumstance of the Revelation or else is the condemnation totally damning? (wisdom or fear is not the question.) Is the poem but a vain speaking, cut off from any and all involvement? Can the poet and his audience make believe? (act differently?) The community loathes the singular distinction. The one that doesn't need its consent. It blends everyone in a collective consciousness. Ignorance is certainly out of place! As long as the well keeps its cover... It is up to the one who speaks to find openings that will clear a path, defying the Law. This is a matter of adroitness and circumstances.

2. Caught in the turmoil, I do not have the time to carefully organize my notes to turn them into a finely-honed communication permitting me to hold forth with ease. As the hour of *the final squawk* approaches, everything happens at once and the difficulty in controlling the tremble of the hand makes the alchemy of the word laughable. There's no more gold. Run for your life! Then the fragment is a stop-gap solution for lead-casting. It permits to record the scraps by avoiding the rigors of argumentation. It is not experimentation with a new genre, or at least not any desire to measure myself with admired authors, but to continue to do with the means at hand.

3. To hold out is the master word. *For the poet all that matters is to catch his breath,* Kateb used to say. He knew how to take a beating from the noble art, and how to feign. At any rate, there's nothing else to do! *In a cat's world, there is no straight line!*

4. Literature and tolerance, literature and revolution not so long ago, literature and…, etcetera. Depending on circumstances, one — this one intentionally vague — demands that literature explain itself or even that it account for itself. One has such demands. For diverse and contradictory reasons, writers accept to play this game, for it is a game; inoffensive most of the time, of slaughter some of the time. Why this complicity?

My experience with writing and a long time spent in the company of poets force me to say that literature is in a very bad state because of these forced and momentarily expedient alliances, being already too tightly strapped into fixed rhetorical frames. The arena is certainly not the ad hoc space of writing, even if some look at it as if it were a bullfight or some other blood sport. The adversary is never at the designed place.

Paradoxically the poet is the one who gets out of the debate because he knows that writing transcends literature. His speaking (son *dit*) breaks the shackles of form and content to approach the essence of original enunciation: the evidence. In this/my/sense, the poet approaches the sacred. Hence the koranic warning against any possible confusion between poetry and divine prophecy. Careful not to mix the registers! And thus the poet is commanded to produce a text that is language *(parole)* and not a saying/speaking *(dire)*. The saying (or writing), because it is fictive, has no reason to be. It can only drag its listener (or reader) along into this valley of the undone where those who are lost err. By saying *(disant)* without doing this voice sows trouble and perturbs the community on its path toward truth. An old bard from the Western part of Algeria, citing the ayât 224 to 227 of the sura *The Poets*, tells me that the river of poetry arrives nowhere (Oued ach-chi'r mâ ywassal); that is why the poet, once mature, owes it to himself to follow the straight line traced by God. Any utterance that does not conform to the divine word falls within the province of satanic illusion. The valley where the poets err is the valley of the unkept promises of Iblis.

5. The quest of writing is individual and free. It presupposes defiance of accepted codes of conduct. Mysticism's undertakings have explored this. The tribe sees in its strange words the gravest danger for its coherence. The tribe is intolerant in that it does not permit the individual to express himself; as far as mysticism is concerned, it only considered the subject the better to merge it with the divine, and then with the brotherhood.

6. What is literature for Algerians? Deep down it does not correspond to a need. Though it be true that man does not live by bread alone, I do not think the other substance to be literature and art. At least not where I come from, and certainly not what is understood today to be literature and art (market? Essence?). It is difficult to admit this to oneself, but it is important not to fool oneself concerning one's society. It is not only the fact of writing in French. No doubt there is a certain marginalization because of the language. Those that have held the power for these last thirty years have never ceased to create this trauma and to keep the writers at bay. This belongs to the difficulties that are surmountable (though they still haven't been!). The core is elsewhere: literature and art are part of entertainment and of the temptation to locate Paradise somewhere on earth again, which is why they can have no future; the latter has been fixed once and for all by the Book, Elsewhere. The poets try to wrest books from the hands of time so as to inscribe themselves into eternity in the present. Can such an activity be tolerated?

"POSTCOLONIAL" NARRATIVE AND IDENTITY: FROM *ORDEAL BY BOW* TO *MOSES' FISH*

I belong to the generation of the Tahar Djaout, Rachid Mimouni, Rabah Belrami, Abdelhamid Laghouati, Youcef Sebti, poets primarily. We did not escape the questioning about identity that tore the country apart. We dealt with it by refusing confinement inside the "false debate" around language, without however occulting the question of language. We all had learned French in school, we used it in our scriptural activities. In everyday orality, each one of us practiced his dialectical speech. I will not elaborate on this given fact, which we lived more or less badly.

At Independence, after his essay "Les zéros tournent en rond," ("The zeros go around in circles") in which he acknowledged the painful exile in the colonizer's language, Malek Haddad condemned himself to silence by discrediting all those who perpetuated colonial alienation by using the French language. This choice of silence to resolve the problem of the "linguistic exile" has served as pretext to stigmatize us. The political regime of the single party system made of the "national language," in fact literal Arabic, the cornerstone of the construction of the nation-state. The writers were ordered to produce works in the "national language," the only language deemed "inhabitable" and that "spoke," that would take charge of the "rediscovered identity" by connecting back to the "fundamental values" of the country.

In the nationalist discourse, the use of French disqualified us offhand from the identity quest given that the latter could express itself only in the Arab language, proclaimed "national language." For the political leaders, obsessed with the unity of the Nation, Algeria was Arab. The recovery of the "national language" was supposed to cement regional idiosyncrasies in a Nation, one and indivisible, following the Jacobin model. The repercussions of such an ideology on writing were dramatic. The "exile" in the language of "dispossession" has given rise to suicidal stands.

Marginal in an "illiterate" society in which writing is not widespread, proscribed by the nationalist discourse, what space can our francophone literature hope for? The Arab-language writers, more and more numerous thanks to the generalization of Arabic as the school language, felt assured that they were in their rights and legitimized by the use of the "national language."

At the end of the sixties, Kateb Yacine brought up the more crucial question of the necessity for the writer to use the vernacular to touch the disenfranchised masses. Neither literary Arabic, nor French were the language spoken in the country. What is a "national language" except the one actually spoken in the country? Kateb Yacine was intent on being in resonance with this language in order to connect with an addressee. He stopped writing in French after he completed *Le Polygone étoilé* which ends on the loss of the "mother tongue:"

After laborious and not very brilliant beginnings, I quickly acquired a taste for the foreign language, and then, deeply in love with a vivacious school teacher, I even went so far as to dream of resolving, for her and without her knowing it, all the problems proposed by my arithmetic textbook!

My mother was too astute not to get disturbed by the infidelity thus committed. I still see her, profoundly vexed, tearing me away from my books — you'll become sick! — then one evening, in a ingenuous voice, but not without sadness, telling me: "as I may no longer distract you from your other world, why don't you teach me the French language..." Thus did the trap of Modern Times close over my fragile roots, and at present I am furious at my stupid pride on the day when, holding a French newspaper, my mother sat down at the table I worked on, distant as never before, pale and silent, as if the cruel school kid's small hand, as he was her son, made it a duty for her to impose the straightjacket of silence on herself, and even to follow him to the end of his effort and solitude — into the lion's den.

Never, even on those days of success with the school teacher, did I stop feeling deep down inside me this second rupture of the umbilical cord, this internal exile that brought the schoolboy closer to his mother only to tear them away, each time a little more, from the murmur of the blood, the reproachful shivering of a language banished, in secret agreement, broken as soon as made...

Thus I had lost at the same time my mother and her tongue, the only unalienable — and yet alienated — treasures!

This concerns a further dimension which I will not develop here, for the mother tongue is not the national language or even the vernacular often monopolized by the fathers.

Kateb Yacine took the path of popular theater to find *an accessible poetic language* and to *speak,* finally.

Mohammed Dib's attitude was exemplary in its refusal to give in to lamentations about either the mother tongue or the vernacular. Rejecting the traps of the linguistic debate, and without making a scene, he took on French as the writing language in which to reconstruct identity in exile — of language and of place. This foothold on exile forces the identity quest to re-interrogate the nationalist tale, to apprehend language in its dimension of translation of speech and to explore the variety of forms in order to open up to the world. By his rectitude and literary exigency Mohammed Dib has encouraged us to persevere in the labor of writing — this alone was worth devoting one's life to — without expecting anything from the literary bazaars.

French was our *spoils of war,* dearly paid for. To fall silent or to continue writing while knowing that the future would belong to the Arab language? Who could foresee the future? Nobody wanted to fall silent because identity and its narrative exceeded the imperatives of a political regime disconnected from the real. The political narrative is a discourse that veils the real; the poetical narrative is the real itself. Confronted with the texts, we had come to understand little by little what was really at stake in writing when it is resolutely in quest of that subtle thing that is the restitution of things and of being, namely that it makes light of language because it is always translation. What is said in writing goes beyond the concern for self-expression of the one who writes because, fundamentally, he does not have the say, but he has to serve a text that always escapes him and that he can only master through a rigorous discipline. The writer begins to know — because Kateb Yacine and Mohammed Dib and Jean Sénac have existed — how words mask, disfigure, distance, transport elsewhere or render mute. The words are always there, welded to the body. They are not the words of the mother, but the words that each writer rediscovers through the exhausting labor of translating that language permeated with the mother tongue that resounds deep down inside him. The ground has been cleared by the founding texts of this francophone literature, those of Mouloud Mammeri, Mouloud Feraoun, Mohammed Dib, Kateb Yacine who had at heart to express the specific identity of the natives in a colonial society. Confronted with the problem of reference, these authors quickly discovered that to write means to inscribe oneself in a tradition of writing, to be able to lean on the "classics" to revisit/(renew) the space of literature, a space of memorial delectation and of commemoration. They tried to open wide an imaginary of homecomings, to insinuate themselves into all the hidden corners of a collective consciousness, to set themselves adrift on the dynamic nostalgia of myth. Which elements of the culture, of aesthetics and of the imagination to deploy to make themselves understood by the French and by their "own people," but before all how to translate everyday reality, still novel, to produce a text that would not be simple curio or ethnographic catalogue? It is in the finesse of the translation that the fate of a literary text is played out, a text capable of expressing all the resonances of the language used and of suggesting, inside the same resonance, the foreclosed space of the occulted language. The colonial situation favored an awareness of the complexity of writing's substratum which cannot be reduced to stylistic operations on a recently acquired language. The accurateness and the efficacy of one's words are a matter neither of the political nor of the documentary, but of a translation that is neither explanation, nor word for word paraphrase. This lesson has served us. That is why, be the written form Arabic or French, the problem of the break with the languages spoken by the people, the mother languages, remains. The language of writing is always a putting into form, a translation. Writing escapes the tongue, it builds its own language without worrying about enriching some particular lexicon.

For me, the question of identity lies at the heart of my work as a writer. It does not, however, arise as a quest for origins — Berber, Arabo-Islamic, Mediterranean or other — or as the recovery of some lost (forever!) property — the authenticity of lineage —, but rather as the recognition/acknowledgment of oneself at the end of the ordeal of writing. That is why the *Odyssey* never ceases to feed my imagination: Ulysses is king of Ithaca. He is the son of Laertes, the father of Telemachus, the husband of Penelope — he knows who he is, from where he comes; he keeps saying it and reminding himself of it in moments of captivity. At the same time, Ulysses is *Nobody*, which allows him to adopt all the personas necessary for his ruses in order to get out of trouble unscathed, without ever losing face, at least that is what he believes. He divulges his name, which he states with pride and even arrogance, only once danger has been averted. His temerity induces him to brandish the signs that could identify him in front of those he loves. Yet his prudence envelops them in fictitious stories. To proceed masked, to scramble all the threads of the narrative while simultaneously desiring to be recognized immediately in all the facets of his identity, is what makes Ulysses suffer and he will be healed only by putting his "good oar" on his shoulder again, once he has overcome the ordeal of the bow. This is so because once arrived home and recognized, one has to leave again for identity to affirm itself. It is this extremely malleable fiction of the Homeric narrative of identity as escape from the reality of the once and forever fixed name that interests me. It forces me to find the adequate narration to give an account of all the upheavals a being and the things that surround it go through in the course of a life. A more or less accomplished crossing. What memory has been able to retain from it. The trace that resists forgetting. Thus narcissism is not in order because the one who looks from the mirror — is it a mirage? — is this other who always slips away at the moment of confrontation, who surprises unexpectedly, lurking in the shadows. This demands a lot of time, patience and skill in ridding oneself of the fallacious rags of seduction to speak unaffectedly (or keep silent) about what happened on the journey, writing being at the end of the day only the return from this *journey to the end of the night*.

Today I am far from having reached some *terra firma* where to take stock but, for having explored several of port of calls, I may humbly hope to arrive somewhere, even if that is nowhere. I am certainly not the most qualified to speak of *The Ordeal of the Bow* or *Moses' Fish*. The texts should be read as they are, I have nothing to add to them. What I can say now is an *à posteriori* gloss. The exercise isn't useless in that it forces me to discuss the formal in a time of crisis and the modalities of narrative to see how the resonances of a text often use the scrambling of the inter-text or reactivate nostalgias of the palimpsest.

The Ordeal of the Bow interrogates the Arab literary form of the *maqamât* while *Moses' Fish* explores classic novelistic fiction, specifically that of Stendhal. The *maqamât* are texts in rhythmed prose, they are playlets or seances during which a truculent character excels in his favorite pastime: tricking people by using every known rhetorical figure. The configuration of the narrative is the circle of the audience which receives and reflects these figures forcing the speaker to make the most extraordinary contortions. Al Harîrî and Al Hamadhâni are considered the masters of the genre. The picaresque novel is said to have its origin in the *maqamât*. *The Ordeal of the Bow* is a text dating back to the end of the eighties.

Why the *maqamât* at that moment? For me at that moment in a country where cant was king it was a matter of revisiting this genre in order to subvert language and of giving free rein to the tricks of discourse when form is illusory. Ten years later, *Moses' Fish,* leaning on a Koranic parable, develops what lies at the fictional core of the Stendhalian novel, namely a hero, a young man who promises a new world. He is the one who crystallizes the current climate while simultaneously not controlling all the givens of his fate. His identity fluctuates. It is in the complex construction of this character that the narrative shapes itself. From then on, the story reveals the arcana of the Hour to the vigilant reader. But I will not say anything more, for it is important to read the books without any commentary to experience their aim without denying the pleasure of reading.

Let us return to identity, to the weft of the narrative and to what is at stake in writing. Form and fiction, while the country is struggling in a murderous national crisis, isn't that a lack of judgment from the part of those who "speak but do not act"?! Thus had the Qur'an condemned the poets. But isn't this anathema itself the refusal to consider the crises as a lack of form and fiction? Instead of the form, the crisis, at least the one we are experiencing in Algeria, develops dis-order and instead of fiction it installs lying. It occults the core of the problem which is that the form and fiction of the war of liberation have become obsolete. Society is suffocating. *O let my keel burst! O let me be gone to the sea!* What does it mean? Simply that writing is true only in as much as it is form and fiction. As such it can investigate the real in order to lay bare its mechanisms, or at least to make these accessible to the imagination. It is because it is form and fiction that it incites us to question. The crisis prevents us from gazing into the distance, it mobilizes all of our energy and ingenuity in useless stratagems for survival. The crisis revels in emphatic figures of discourse and fears nothing more than free speech anchored in a libertarian heritage. Form is never devoid of content, it is worked through by its content. It dilates content and liberates all its potentialities to allow the pleasure listening to it gives us. Form permits content to reach its goal, namely to procure the jubilation listening gives us. Fiction, for its part, breaks open the partitions of the real by forcing the reader to question himself concerning the truth of the story.

The post-colonial situation is interesting only if it projects the colonized onto the world stage rather than locking him inside the cramped borders of the independent nation. This projection, however, in no way signifies the abandonment of the quest for identity. It is not a question of positioning oneself voluntarily inside "universal literature" — avatar of globalization or consequence of the unequal configuration of the literary field? — while distancing oneself from the questionings of "one's own" (those never abandon one of theirs!). The universal is not the elsewhere: the former comes within the province of the order of the world, while the latter derives from the imaginary, but both are indispensable for the unfolding of a reconciled identity. They are fictions whose form has to be searched for on paths apart from the artifice of the moment. This approach demands a humility proportionate with the ambition of the work. Then a writing may emerge in which the other does not speak otherly anymore except to interrogate what animates each one of us. He is no longer stuck in a neurotic dialectic where the eye collides with a distorting mirror. He can finally look everywhere. Meet other open gazes where a sharing and a confrontation of forms and themes can work itself out. For the tragic experience of the colonized, it too, can lead to a chant indispensable for the organization of the world. For lack of producing this chant, all the suffering will have been in vain!

WITH JEAN SÉNAC

The Noûn! (Who exactly says?)
A trace of God on the nail. But God, but the nail?
—Jean Sénac, *Diwân du Noûn (xorpoème)*

September 1973… Today, thirty years have gone by…
This sadness always, always, of things not done!
We had an appointment that day. I was coming from Barika. The Hodna.
I had a four-day furlough and used it for a quick trip to Algiers. To breathe.
Barika, that's Biribi! That's where the hotheads and the deserters were re-formed. Leitmotiv of the Secretary General of the daïra, Si Mohammed, who had read Darien. I was absolving my military service working for the Agrarian Revolution. It was a bit rough, but more bearable than the Green Barrier in N'Gaous.

Opening *El Moudjahid*, I learn of your death.

I sat down on the first still practicable public bench. I was walking up rue Didouche on my way to your place.

… I stayed there for a long time. Like a freeze frame. Then movement picked up again. I scribbled on the front page of the newspaper. I didn't know what to do any longer in this city overcome by grayness. *A city of thistles.*

> City stranger
> wakes up at the foot of day
> wearing make-up to turn
> my head

> To forget your gaze bullet-proof immigrant

> I sat myself down on a public bench to take my hair loss
> for a walk

The white square

And the dead

Since that time, the dead have not stopped harassing me... Fate practices black humor and derision. The death of the poet remains trivial despite the objectivity of (or because of) chance.
I had so much to learn from Jean and now he disappears without a warning!
...

To write... Witnesses... I see friends who have known him better than I did: Alain Rais, Malek Alloula, Hamid Tibouchi or the Benanteurs. On occasion someone will bring him up. Paradoxically, the more time passes, the more he comes up in our conversations. The events make his presence necessary.

I was fifteen. Sénac was signing his volume of poems *Matinale de mon peuple*. He had signed a copy for my father. That was in Paris, just after Independence. For the first time in my life I saw a live poet. Leafing through the book, the shock that it wasn't Victor Hugo, Musset or Vigny! Poetry could be written like this. No rhymed verses. Everyday words, no need for a dictionary to look up their meanings. A simple syntax.
Poetry is the gaze without rancor of the poor man. It is also his fist.
My eyes opened wide! And yet, it looked very serious.

... First of all, poetry is life. I hear it. Louder and louder. No puns.
A panoply of blue, of urine and of solid gold. No matter how you lay out the words. It is your flesh and your blood without mystery.
I had read him, of course.
Jean flung this at me in a discussion on texts that I had sent him. His opinion mattered a lot to me. There were many of us who sought him out. He would answer with a mix of seriousness and irony...

He, a transferrer, who flushed things out, in a country crowing over revolution. (Not the one that scares!)... He knew how to gather the most diverse people. Around him, explosive vortexes. Slow-burning fuses too. (Fuses that would peter out, too???)

He introduced me to Hamid Tibouchi, I have a very precise memory of our first encounter in *the cellar,* and to many other poets...

His beard helped! The kids in the street called him *Boulahya,* the bearded man. He was someone they respected.

Noûn. The formula from the diwân is not a formulaic recipe. *Poetry passes!* The poet has nothing to prove. He has to live and account for that life, his life. All poets aspire to this. So, what formula?

When I met him, he cut holes into the white page. "You see, my universe is already made. What's left for me to do is to dig in order to explore all the hidden recesses..." Memory holes, *a life full of holes,* ass-holes, to make one's hole, to end up in the hole...

He also had a bottle of lemonade he saved: "This *gazouse,* I keep it for Boumedienne if he decides to come and visit me. The first step is up to him..." Meanwhile...
... The leader had other priorities.

I saw him often.
Every weekend... the instruction period, after the initial forty-five days. I spent my Saturday-Sundays prancing about from Passage Calmels to Boulevard Mohammed V to the rue Elysée Reclus...
Mohammed Khadda, Mustapha Kaïd and Jean Sénac were my elders.
I had landed. Will-o'-the-wisp in the storm zone.
Thanks to them I was able to find my bearings in the city. To map out my anguish. It was the era of the socialist management of companies but already the loved one was no longer as *beautiful as a committee...*

In Cherchell, the distribution of the mails was awaited with impatience... Each week I would get a letter from Sénac. In the middle of the week. That enabled me to hold out until the weekend furlough...

I have lost these letters during my peregrinations. I have kept only one letter together with its envelope. For my birthday Sénac sent me a postcard with Baya's taos bird to decorate my locker and a 10-dinar note to feast in the mess. The stamp on the envelope carries Uncle Hô's effigy.

What Sénac taught me *(that an ode isn't written with words alone)* took me some time to realize.

DATES OF COMPOSITION & ACKNOWLEDGMENTS

Poetry

Title	Date of composition	Publisher & Date
L'arc et la cicatrice		Editions de la Différence, 2006
Café Marine (Lettres)	(1978)	
Chaume, noue et tôle		
Gravité de l'Ange		Editions de la Différence, 2004
Le radeau de la mémoire		
Schistes de Tahmad 2	(1982)	
Etats de chose suivi de *Fatras*	(1991–1994)	La Rumeur des Ages, 2003
Cinq mouvements de l'âme		
Fatras		
Traverser	(1992–1993)	La Rumeur des Ages, 2002
(3 sections)		
La Sandale d'Empédocle	(1992–2006)	
Ce Tatar-là 2	(1997–1998)	Launay Rollet, Editions Dana, 2000
Épreuve 2	(1998–1999)	Launay Rollet, Editions Dana, 2002
Césure	(2001–2002)	Wigwam, 2006
Retraite	(2004)	Le Bec en l'air, 2004
(with photography by Olivier de Sépibus)		
L'ancêtre cinéphile	(1983–2006)	Editions de la Différence, 2010

Prose

Sultan Galiev	(1972–1977)	Sindbad, 1985
Le Vieux de la Montagne Revised edition	(1977–1981)	Sindbad, 1983 la Différence, 2008
L'Épreuve de l'Arc	(1982–1989)	Sindbad, 1990
Gens de Mosta "Ulysse chez les intégristes" "Nécrologie"	(1990–1994)	Actes Sud/Sindbad, 1997
Le Poisson de Moïse	(1994–2001)	Editions Paris-Méditerranée, 2001
Le Maître de l'heure	(2008)	La Différence, 2008

Essays

Insert (introduction to *Le Maître de l'Heure*)
in *Dans le Soulevement*   Editions de la Différence, 2012

    Le Surréalism Maghrébin
    Le témoin indésirable
    Évocation du raï
    Le ventre est encore fécond
    Vallée de d'inaccompli
    Narration et identité "post-coloniale"
    Avec Jean Sénac

HABIB TENGOUR, poet and anthropologist, born 1947 in Mosta-
ganem (Algeria), lives and works between Constantine & Paris. Consid-
ered as one of the Maghrib's most forceful and visionary poetic voices of
the post-colonial era, Tengour, who authored a "Manifesto of Maghribian
Surrealism" in 1981, explores the Algerian & Maghribi cultural space in
all its ramifications — oral & hagiographic traditions, popular imagination
& founding myths, collective memory, raï music & the lived experiences
of exile — in some eight books of prose & twelve collections of poetry to
date. He also translates from English (P. Joris) & from Arabic (Saadi
Youssef, Chawki Abdelamir) & has just completed the anthology *Poems
for the Millennium, Volume 4: The University of California Book of North
African Literature,* in collaboration with Pierre Joris.

Poet, essayist, anthologist & translator PIERRE JORIS' most recent pub-
lications are a translation, *The Meridian: Final Version—Drafts—Materials*
by Paul Celan, the poem sequence *Canto Diurno #4: The Tang Extending
from the Blade, Justifying the Margins: Essays 1990–2006,* & *Aljibar I &
II* (poems). A gathering of essays on Joris' poetry & translations, edited
by Peter Cockelbergh under the title *Pierre Joris: Topographies of the In-
between,* has just been published by Literaria Pragensia. With Habib Ten-
gour he edited *Poems for the Millennium, Volume 4: The University of
California Book of North African Literature,* to be published in late 2012
by University of California Press.

TITLES FROM BLACK WIDOW PRESS

TRANSLATION SERIES

Approximate Man and Other Writings
by Tristan Tzara. Translated and edited
by Mary Ann Caws.

Art Poétique by Guillevic.
Translated by Maureen Smith.

The Big Game by Benjamin Péret.
Translated with an introduction by
Marilyn Kallet.

Capital of Pain by Paul Eluard.
Translated by Mary Ann Caws, Patricia
Terry, and Nancy Kline.

Chanson Dada: Selected Poems
by Tristan Tzara. Translated with an
introduction and essay by Lee Harwood.

*Essential Poems and Writings of Joyce
Mansour: A Bilingual Anthology*
Translated with an introduction by
Serge Gavronsky.

*Essential Poems and Prose of
Jules Laforgue*
Translated and edited by Patricia Terry.

*Essential Poems and Writings of
Robert Desnos: A Bilingual Anthology*
Edited with an introduction and essay
by Mary Ann Caws.

EyeSeas (Les Ziaux)
by Raymond Queneau. Translated with an
introduction by Daniela Hurezanu and
Stephen Kessler.

Furor and Mystery & Other Writings
by René Char. Edited and translated by
Mary Ann Caws and Nancy Kline.

The Inventor of Love & Other Writings
by Gherasim Luca. Translated by Julian
and Laura Semilian. Introduction by
Andrei Codrescu. Essay by Petre Răileanu.

La Fontaine's Bawdy
by Jean de la Fontaine. Translated with
an introduction by Norman R. Shapiro.

Last Love Poems of Paul Eluard
Translated with an introduction by
Marilyn Kallet.

Love, Poetry (L'amour la poésie)
by Paul Eluard. Translated with an essay
by Stuart Kendall.

*Poems of André Breton:
A Bilingual Anthology*
Translated with essays by Jean-Pierre
Cauvin and Mary Ann Caws.

Poems of A.O. Barnabooth
by Valéry Larbaud. Translated by
Ron Padgett and Bill Zavatsky.

Preversities: A Jacques Prévert Sampler
Translated and edited by Norman R.
Shapiro.

The Sea and Other Poems by Guillevic.
Translated by Patricia Terry. Introduction
by Monique Chefdor.

To Speak, to Tell You?
Poems by Sabine Sicaud. Translated by
Norman R. Shapiro. Introduction and
notes by Odile Ayral-Clause.

forthcoming translations

*Essential Poems and Writings of
Pierre Reverdy*
Edited by Mary Ann Caws. Translated
by Mary Ann Caws, Patricia Terry,
Ron Padgett, and John Ashbery.

A Life of Poems, Poems of a Life by Anna
de Noailles. Translated by Norman R.
Shapiro. Introduction by Catherine Perry.

MODERN POETRY SERIES

WWW.BLACKWIDOWPRESS.COM

This book was set primarily in Sabon, with
Grit Primer for the title pages and cover.

Sabon is an oldstyle serif typeface de-
signed by German-born typographer and
designer Jan Tschichold (1902–1974). He
crafted Sabon as a font that modernized
the classics and honed each letter's fine de-
tails, particularly the evenness of the serifs.

Grit Primer is a distressed, aged type-
face resurrected from letterpress samples
of schoolhouse primers common around
the turn of the century.